ENCOUNTERS STUPIDITY AND DESTINY

G. A. BECKETT

ENCOUNTERS STUPIDITY AND DESTINY

© G. A. BECKETT

First published June 2021

ISBN: 978-0-6488738-8-4 Paperback

ISBN: 978-0-6488738-9-1 E-Book

All rights reserved. Without limiting the rights under copyright reserved above, no part of this publication may be reproduced, stored in or introduced into a database and retrieval system or transmitted in any form or by any means (electronic, mechanical, photocopying, recording or otherwise) without the prior written permission of the owner of the copyright.

DISCLAIMER

This book is memoir. It reflects the author's present recollections of experiences over time. Some names and characteristics have been changed, some events have been compressed, and some dialogue has been recreated. This is a work of fiction. Although its form is that of an autobiography, it is not one. Space and time have been rearranged to suit the convenience of the book, and with the exception of public figures, any resemblance of persons living or dead is coincidental. The opinions expressed are those of the characters and should not be confused with the author's.

CONTENTS

Australian Exit (The Beginning). 1
Manila. 8
Ferry Trip. 14
Meeting Cherry. 23
Plantation Bay Stay. 29
Bohol Trip. 39
Manila Hotel. 49
Thailand Trip. 59
Saigon. 66
Knee Operation. 73
Japan Trip. 77
Months in Australia. 82
Japan Return Trip. 85
Korea. 96
Cavite Manila. .100
Luzon Travel and Bridal Boutique. 103
Marriage and Birth of My Son. 111
Baptism Party in Alona Beach Bohol. 118
Bridal Boutiques and Fashion Design Course. 122

Cherry and her Boyfriend. 126

Hong Kong. 133

London and Paris. 138

Life in Cebu and My Arrest. 148

Jail. 152

Vanuatu. 157

Makati Burgos Street Meeting and Travels. 162

Cebu Court Hearing. 167

Bay Gardens Manila and Another Court Case. 171

Singapore. 179

Bangkok And Pattaya. 186

Singapore Return and Engagement. 193

You Me Her at Phuket. 198

Manila and Mindoro Island. 204

Las Vegas-Our Wedding. 209

Honeymoon In The USA. 216

Canada, Bahamas and More of USA. 220

London and Europe. 225

Baltic Cruise and Russia. 230

Chapter 1

AUSTRALIAN EXIT (THE BEGINNING).

The sun rose early on a hotter than hot Australian summer's day. It was January 13, at the turn of the new millennium. My second marriage to Pamela was now over, and for whatever reason, I stupidly married this woman in the first place will always confuse and bewilder me. After I learned that Pamela was just a gold digger with a split personality, all while being a very good drama actress, there was no reason for me to stay; but one thing that is now positively sure is that the marriage was now finished.

You could ask what happened to my marriage and how it all ended. Well, my answer to that is, I guess, I am not the most perfect man out there, but then again, who is? And maybe I did drink a little more excessively than I should have, but at least I was peaceful and happy when I drank. It was much better than having to endure my ex-wife's erratic behavior while sober. I was basically choosing to drink over dealing with her, and trust me, you would have done the same. I mean, this woman who is now erased from my future life (hopefully) was a total psychotic!

She suffered from extreme bipolar tantrums and whenever the personality of another demonic woman inside her body surfaced, I would quickly hide all the knives in the kitchen. I had to find a hiding spot where Pamela the Demon could not find them, in fear of what she might do - especially to me. Pamela the Demon - I gave this name to her second personality, and I wouldn't be surprised if there actually was a demon living inside her body all along. Maybe I am a little sad; not because our marriage is over, but for the next victim she would go on to trap.

Looking back on the past, my most vivid memory is coming home one day and seeing Pamela squatting, chanting in a strange tongue. There were words not known by human ears, at least not by mine. Entrenched in her demonic hands was a large knife, and when she saw me at the entrance of the room, she immediately stopped her ritual, or whatever it was, and stared at me. In a split second, she got up and started running towards me, wielding this knife in her hand violently while screaming like a possessed woman. The whole scenario was definitely as bad as it sounds, if not worse. At that time, I backed up and quickly ran out of the house, avoiding her swiping weapon. When I successfully made it to the car, I stayed inside nervously all night, with the windows and doors locked securely. She had even taken hold of the whole house to herself! And seeing Pamela the Demon awakened, there was no way I was going back into that Maze of Doom - at least, not for the night. The house might as well have been turned into Hell.

Spending the whole night in my car, which was far from the comfort of my bed, and also the fear of Pamela the Demon launching yet another weapon at me anytime I let my guard down, I couldn't get even a wink of sleep. The next morning, terrified yet curious as to what was happening inside, I entered the house slowly and cautiously. To my relief, the maniac inside the split personality of this woman was now hiding, replaced by a person that greeted me with a smile, "Good morning!" As sweet as these words were, they made me feel even more terrified. A totally different person had now surfaced and taken over the Demon. Apart from the fact that my heart was hammering in my chest, it was all really confusing to me. I never knew when the other demon personality would surface again, and I could never be sure of what this personality was capable of - although I had a fair idea from this frightening experience. Nevertheless, this nightmare relationship was now finally over, and I was free to move on with my life. Thank God, or whatever force it was that let this happen, I could now live without the constant fear of being stabbed by a knife every single day. Perhaps, this also allowed Pamela the Demon to move on.

Today is the day I will fly off to my future destiny, hopeful to start a new life all over again. If only I had known what the next ten years would bring, maybe I would have stayed and never left Australia. But then again, maybe I wouldn't have; maybe I would have just done things a lot smarter, knowing what transpired. Over the next ten years, I would say, I was likened to a plane or train running out of control as the person at the wheel or throttle was far too inexperienced to control the unexpected obstacles that were ahead and experience would be needed to be steer through these mishaps.

My life over the next decade would take more twists and turns than a fun park roller coaster. I couldn't even have begun to imagine what was waiting for me, even in my wildest dreams. So, this is my story - it may be a little insane, but we cannot plan life and play it the way we want now, can we? Things just happen, and I cannot look back and dwell on whatever I could have done differently but didn't. I need to keep going forever onward, finding new paths and new beginnings. My only comment can be, well, that did not go exactly as I had planned! Even today, I feel like the end of the roller coaster ride was maybe worth it after all. So, all I can say if you continue to read on is have an open mind, and don't forget to tighten up your seatbelt!

Arriving at Brisbane Airport, I hurriedly dropped off my hired car and hastily returned the keys to the Hertz desk on the second floor of the Terminal Building. I thanked the warmly smiling attendant, whose smile was far too contagious that I found myself smiling as well. I took a good look at her again and it seemed like she knew something that I didn't. Maybe it was her eyes as if trying to talk and I heard the word "beware". Of course, that couldn't be true. I moved on, believing it to just be my imagination - or, was it? It was now time to check in my bags at the Qantas section on the third floor, just one extra floor above Hertz. After a short wait in line, this chore was all done and completed. Now, I had my boarding pass held tightly in my hand for my flight to Manila Philippines, for my new start, towards my new life.

Then, I proceeded down to the departure area, ready to set to the new journey ahead. After finishing all my customs and security checks without any delays or problems, I once again felt and noticed warm smiles all around me - from the customs officers to the security guards. And just like the smile and eyes of the Hertz attendant, these eyes also seemed to talk. However, the mixtures of different voices made it unclear for me to translate, or even understand, their words. Did they know something? Was I just happy? Or was it just a little paranoia encroaching on my thoughts?

Ignoring the untranslatable words from the voices after all there was nothing else that I could do, I continued on and walked past the duty-free shop. I checked the alcohol and was happy to see a special on Vintage Moet Champagne. I still enjoyed drinking, though not as excessively as before. Seeing my favorite brands of alcohol always made me feel excited. Even though the allowance at Manila was only two bottles, I stocked up with four bottles. I wanted to take my chances in the Philippines as I was sure that no one would really care, even if I had twenty bottles of champagne. So, four bottles seemed more than sufficient for my trip.

As if the drinks weren't enough, the aromatic smell of coffee lured me. I was aroused by the aroma which invited me or rather forced me, to purchase a hot cup of Café Latte. As much as I enjoyed drinking, hot cups of coffee gave me a certain sense of fulfillment and satisfaction. The sweet scent wasn't something I could just ignore, no matter where I was. So, there I was, with a hot Café Latte in my hand and nervousness and excitement in my mind. The latter crawled quickly to my hand, which was holding the hot cup, and made me spill some of the delicious drink. My hand started to burn but I was unfazed, as I quite often encountered this problem when drinking hot coffee.

I didn't realize how quickly time was passing, and soon, I heard the loudspeaker advise all the passengers not to board as it was only a pre-boarding announcement. Why exactly the airline felt the need to announce that was something I could only wonder about. Anyway, before long, the next thing I heard was yet again another announcement. I sighed but, this time, it was a boarding announcement which was an actual boarding announcement. So, naturally, all of the passengers rushed to the plane, pushing and shoving recklessly on their way, as though the plane was going to depart without them. Whatever it was, somehow, they felt that the pushing was needed. As for me, I was just relaxing with my delicious hot coffee in my just as much burning hand. Ignoring the commotion of people rushing and pushing each other, I looked down at my hand and noticed the bright red scald marks from the spillage. Oh well, that was to be expected.

I continued drinking and was enjoying the drink until all the passengers had gone. Only then did I get up and slowly walked down the boarding tunnel onto the plane, inhaling the plane fumes along the way that slowly made their way into my head. My mind kept repeating the words, it's time to start over! I was far too excited, I guess. I found my way onto my seat and after what seemed like only minutes, the plane took off. It started by the engines roaring and sped then down the tarmac. When the wheels of the 747 lifted off and the plane flew, so did my excitement.

I was now excited than ever for the unknown adventure and the new experiences I was going to gather, and maybe cherish, through this trip; I was curious about what was to transpire. Some would ask why specifically did I decide to visit Manila, and I would say that is because I wanted to visit a good friend, Vic Diaz, who was also an old Philippine actor, or maybe that I wanted to visit the beaches. But truthfully, honestly, and quite frankly, the real reason was the beautiful Filipina that was luring me to this crazy country.

Anyhow, the reason why I was sitting on this plane is not important or crucial to the story. We must just remember "life is the longest thing we will ever do". I was comfortably reclined in my seat, relaxing and waiting for what was to come ahead when two waitresses approached my seat. They asked me if I would like anything to drink, to which I courteously said, "A XXXX beer, please." It was the Queensland local beer that I suddenly had a craving for. What trip would it be if I didn't have anything to drink? Once the waitress handed me the beer, I laid back and sipped on my beer while chewing on some peanuts that the friendly staff had given me with the beer. The first movie was now starting on the big screen at the front of the plane. Curious to see what it was, and also to satiate my boredom, I placed my headset over my ears and set my eyes on the screen. The movie playing was called Men in Black and I quite enjoyed it. At that moment, I was feeling like the king of the world – drinking beer while watching a movie 36,000 feet above the earth.

After the movie ended, the waitresses started serving lunch and, me being quite hungry, I devoured the feast with a little red wine which actually tasted more like vinegar than wine. Nevertheless, I didn't complain and just drank it all, imagining as if I was enjoying a magnificent French Red Wine from the Bordeaux regions of France. That made me feel a little better about the taste.

The flight was smooth and peaceful after that. After lunch, they started the second movie - which was Pulp Fiction, a classic Quentin Tarantino movie. Needless to say, I enjoyed this one too. Thanks to the smooth flight, comfortable seating, and friendly staff, the seven-hour flight went by fast. After two movies on the big screen, some tasty food, and a few beers, before I knew it, the Captain announced in a firm but courteous voice, "We are now descending into Manila." In a few minutes, he spoke again, "Please fasten your seatbelts for the final descent." Now, my journey was actually starting. The arrival was now imminent, and my heart almost leapt out of my chest as the wheels touched down.

Chapter 2

MANILA.

Once we were on the ground and out of the plane, I proceeded to the immigration desk. As customary, I placed a 500 Peso note inside my passport, and using my friendly voice, I said, "Can I have a balikbayan visa please, Sir?" I needed longer than the usual three weeks that are given to arriving passengers, hence the little bonus. A little bonus to this humble elderly immigration officer, and everyone is a winner. The immigration officer smiled at me, took the bribe, and said, "Enjoy your holiday!" I was delighted that the bribe worked, and to show my delight, I decided to reply in his native language. "Salamat Sir, Ingat Ka Palagi," was what I replied - a common expression in the country. In case you are wondering, it means "Thank you, and Take Care Always" in English.

After immigration, I went on to pick up my one and only old suitcase, which, looking at my bag on the carousel, looked like the dirtiest and ugliest bag. I noticed how unattractive it looked, and despite that, when one lady asked me if that was my bag, I proudly said, "Yes, madam". The next thing to do was clearing customs once again. This time, the officers were yet again giving me that smile I had come to know all too well. They said nothing about my duty-free bag with the bottles of champagne that I had bought before in Australia. Why didn't they? Well, maybe they did not know, or really just did not care, what the limit on alcohol was. As long as a visitor to their country was happy, that was all that really mattered to them.

Outside the airport, I could smell the stench in the air from pollution. Manila is a very over-crowded city. The struggles and hardships these people endured - I could not even begin to imagine. Thinking about this was saddening, but by blocking these thoughts from my mind, the smell made me happy, though a deep breath would make me cough. In the airport in Manila, there were no public taxis. They didn't even allow visitors inside the airport, so the simplest and easiest way to travel from the airport was to hire a prepaid car. On arrival, I had to exchange some Australian money for Philippine pesos to buy a ticket for the journey from the office of the car company to the city, I had to travel in the hired car. Before long, my bag was loaded into the boot of the white Toyota, and off we drove!

After an hour of chaos on the road, I finally arrived at the Hyatt Hotel on Roxas Boulevard. I checked into the hotel, showered, and even though it had been a long day, the clock on the wall read 9:15pm. It was far too early for me to go to bed; I was too excited to sleep this early. I remembered that the time in Manila was two hours behind Brisbane time, which would now be 11:15pm. Having nothing to do, I found myself in the hotel elevator and descended downstairs to the hotel bar where I ordered a San Miguel beer - it was the local Philippine beer. Now was the time to unwind.

The barman was named Boyz, and all the waitresses looked happy with warm smiles on their faces. Perhaps that was the thing I liked most about this country; all the people were friendly even in this poverty-stricken country. They never dwell on things and just accept their simple life as it is. One of the waitresses that caught my eye was Suzy, or at least that was what it read on her shiny silver nametag.

Not only was she a beauty queen, but it seemed like she was enjoying my flirty attitude as much as I was enjoying flirting with her. We talked for a while and boy; I was sure that she would taste better than the food that was served on my Qantas flight! However, being a realist, I knew she was far too wise. A man who wanted to sniff her sweet panties was going to have to come up with a lot more than just a bit of sweet talk. So, I never went farther than just some flirting here and there.

In the background, love songs were melodically flowing from the very talented piano player, and the singer had a very well-trained voice. For me, it was a very upmarket bar - full of expensive girls with expensive tastes. It was not what I was looking for. I then decided it was time to explore. So, I said my farewell to the bar and went out for a walk. After only a ten-minute walk from my hotel, I found a group of bars called - The Complex.

Even though the walk was short, I was starting to sweat because of my alcohol intake. Arriving at this destination, I entered this temptation complex and shot a prolonged gaze inside the first club. In all honesty, I was amazed at what I saw. This bar of temptation comprised of a stage that was full of young and beautiful girls. The youngest girl, more like an angel lookalike, was maybe eighteen and the oldest looked twenty-five. Some of these beauties were smiling, some looked sad, and others had distant looks on their young and pretty faces. For whatever reason they were here, it did not really deserve my analysis or judgment. I was just happy that they were there. And I was happy I was there, as well.

I had seen this type of bar before, but that was a lifetime ago - or so it seemed. Maybe, in reality, it had been about one year. So, of course, I felt like I was in heaven. All I could see were angels, or at least something very similar.

My feelings were only an idiot would refuse to go inside and give up the opportunity to enjoy the beauty of heaven. Without too much persuasion, I found myself sitting inside this palace of temptation and drinking yet another cold San Miguel beer. Besides me, three beauties were now sitting there, who looked nothing less than angels. They noticed me and started telling me how young and handsome I looked. Knowing full well that Filipino girls hardly ever lie, I thought it must be true. In contrast or reality, these girls were professional liars. They were trained to milk every last drop of money they could get from a customer. These girls were experts at that, so much so that they knew full well that playing on a middle-aged man's ego would hopefully get them invited to their hotel for the night. Even though it felt like a dream to me, it was total reality. At least, for the night, I would live the fantasy, anyway. Well, of course, it was only the beginning of yet another trap that would lead me into a world of temptation and non-thinking stupidity for the next ten years.

Midnight arrived quickly, and after a long day, it was now time to get back to the hotel for a good sleep. And even though the girls were tempting, I eventually went to bed alone. I had plenty of time to catch a fish for my aquarium some other day. I woke up the next day in the early morning and slept like I was knocked unconscious by a Mike Tyson punch. My ears were still ringing from the engines of the plane, but that was nothing a shower couldn't fix! After taking a hot shower, I was feeling fresh again and was ready to move on to the next chapter of my life. Although yesterday had been a very long day, I felt no ill effects from my travels; no jet lag or anything. Maybe it was the smell of freedom or the happiness of meeting my friend again for breakfast, but I was positive and had a feeling of positivity surging through my body.

Soon, I received a call from my friend, informing me that he had arrived. So, I preceded downstairs where I met up with my old friend, Vic. His smiling face always made me happy and feel positive. Vic was a joker and had absolutely no hair on his head. He had large eyes and only three teeth in the front of his mouth. These three perfectly good teeth were enough for him, which he would use to hold cigarettes between. The locals always recognized him for his past movie roles in Tagalog movies. He was known to always play the bad guys, or villains, in all of his movies - he would either play as a drug dealer, a rapist, or a murderer. And even though he could act well as these characters, his actual personality was the total opposite from his movie roles. In reality, he was a kind and caring family man.

When I arrived downstairs, I saw Vic smiling and joking with about eight of the hotel staff who had come to recognize him. I had met Vic years earlier in Australia, where he used to come to buy racehorses from one of my friends as his agent. My friend would deliver the horses to Vic in Manila., and that's how I came to know Vic. After greeting each other, we both sat down at a table nearest to the window of the hotel restaurant. We talked and laughed while eating a magnificent buffet breakfast and reminisced about many things from the past. I also discussed my present and told him about my plans: I was going to catch Super Ferry 12 to Cebu tomorrow. I had also made a booking at a Mactan Island Resort for four days, which was called Plantation Bay. After enjoying and finishing the delicious breakfast, I said my goodbyes to Vic for now. We both knew that we would meet again in the not-too-distant future.

I felt great and refreshed after spending some time with Vic. He was always a delight to meet up and chat with! Even his fans would agree. So, my plans for the remainder of the day included preparing for my ferry trip. I had a good gym workout, and the sweat I had afterward was so much that I could only guess that it was water retention from all the beers I had drunk the previous day. After the workout, I went off to the hotel beauty parlor where I enjoyed a haircut, shave, manicure, pedicure, and massage. Walking out, I felt great and even more refreshed than before. The Filipinos were treating me really well with their ever-smiling faces and their warm gestures. There was nothing for me to regret about coming to this country. Or so I thought.

After a very professional yet inexpensive service at the hotel beauty parlor, I felt happy to leave a little tip to the friendly workers. So, I did. I planned to go to bed early since tomorrow morning is another day with unknowns ahead, with my planned sea voyage to Cebu City.

Chapter 3

FERRY TRIP.

It was early morning on a Sunday when I was abruptly awoken by the loud buzzing of the hotel phone. Still half asleep, I reached over and answered the phone. "This is your wake-up call, Sir," the voice on the other end said, which I was not sure was whether it was the voice of a human or if it was computer-generated. Nevertheless, I replied with a "Thank you" to the mysterious voice on the other end. Brushing off the mystery of the voice on the phone, I gathered my thoughts and was now wide awake after a deep sleep.

Even though I was very excited to get up for my Ferry trip, I lay momentarily on my comfortable bed for a few minutes. I then rose slowly from my bed, the first thing I did after a shower was packed up my things for the trip in my old faithful bag. I had to make sure that nothing was left behind so it took a little longer than usual to get organized, but I wasn't going to be late for the trip. After packing all my possessions, I took my final elevator ride downstairs and checked out of the hotel. My excitement was hitting the roof at this point. Maybe I was feeling it a little more than usual because it had been a while since I went on a boat trip. Needless to say, I was looking forward to what this day would bring.

For my journey to the Ferry, I had to hire a hotel car. After loading my old bag and getting myself in the car, we proceeded to the Terminal which was located near Tondo. Luckily, it was a Sunday morning. In Manila, this was the day when the traffic on the normally busy roads was pretty much non-existent. Driving on the empty road, I looked out of the car window and it felt like a strange phenomenon; it was almost eerie to be traveling without hearing the loud horns of passing vehicles on the road. The roads on Sundays were empty because this was a catholic country - Sunday was the day of rest, as it says that in the Bible. We also didn't have to constantly stop the ride because of thick bustling traffic, so I felt more positivity surging through the day. Maybe it was going to be a good trip because of the positive signs.

The hotel car driver was extremely polite, just like all of the other staff I had talked to ever since coming to this country. Recognizing me as a foreigner, he thoughtfully informed me that this Port was not a safe area, since he knew I wouldn't be familiar with this place I took notice of his advice as he was a local, and heeded his warning. After checking in for the journey, I just stayed inside the Ferry Terminal to stay safe, remembering the driver's concern. Fortunately, I had no problems and didn't run into any danger either. Then, after waiting for some time, it was time to go onboard. I boarded the Super Ferry 12, which was owned by Aboitiz Company at the time. I was really excited about the twenty-one-hour trip to Cebu and planned to enjoy these hours as much as I could. After all, I deserved that much after what I had to go through.

Cebu City is commonly known as the Queen City of the South and is the capital of the Visayas Region of the Philippines. If only I had known that I would meet my future wife aboard this boat, I would have never made this trip in the first place. A woman who was a very well disguised devil wasn't something I was looking forward to meeting on this trip, but there I was, climbing the three floors of stairs which led to my room onboard this magnificent Ferry.

It was a long and steep walk to board the vessel, climbing up three flights of stairs with hundreds of passengers pushing and shoving on this slow climb to the top. It reminded me of the scenario back at Brisbane airport when passengers were rushing and shoving down their way to their seats. At that time, I was sitting down and relaxing while waiting for my turn. Here, I had to blend in with this impatient crowd - though I did not mirror their methods of pushing and shoving. I remembered the sweet scent and taste of the Café Latte I had back at the airport and I looked down at my hand that the coffee had spilled over; the burn mark was fading away. Well, I still had the bottles of champagne from then in my bag. I hoped for better experiences and stories on my way ahead. "YOLO" (You Only Live Once) - was a thought that entered my head while climbing the stairs.

The boat I was getting on was huge, almost the size of a cruise boat. Though, of course, it was not that luxurious. Still, it didn't feel so far below that standard. My room onboard was a suite room. So, after collecting my keys from the courteous desk staff, I was then escorted to my room like a VIP. They also carried my bag and once again, I felt like a king - this time not in the sky, but on waters. Could this get any better? When we arrived in my room, my escort showed me all the features and services I had already available. The inside of the room looked great; it had everything I needed to get by the day, even if I didn't get out of my room at all. There was a cable TV, a double bed, a desk, and even a refrigerator in which I placed one of the four bottles of Vintage Moet. They were still in my suitcase from when I had bought them at Brisbane Airport for the trip. To say I was happy would be an understatement at this point. I loved the room, the boat, and my life at the time. It was the moment when I could say that this trip was worth it, and there was nothing that could ever change my mind about this, or so I thought. I was becoming even more excited now for my boat ride ahead, the lunch announcement was called. Food is always a first to a good ride ahead! Luckily, without too much trouble, I found the restaurant where the food was being served. Yet again, I found myself too happy and content with this trip, and the food did not disappoint me or made me feel any less happy.

I was served the popular Filipino dish that they called Chicken Adobo. It was also served with rice. I would say, as a tourist in the Philippines, that the dish was "Masarap" - which is Tagalog for delicious. By now, my Tagalog vocabulary was increasing day by day, and the more I improved, the more I knew that it would come to be an advantage in times ahead. I finished my lunch quickly and left a clean plate where once it was filled with delicious food. I could get used to this. After eating to my fullest, it was now time to explore. So, I got up with a full stomach and a happy, excited mood to my next destination. At this point, I was sure there would be nothing that could disappoint me.

The first thing I did after lunch was going to the top outside deck, where I could watch the Ferry pull away from Manila Bay. It was emitting a loud deafening horn now, blowing to signal that we were leaving. Standing on the top deck, I watched a crowd of locals running to the boat, crying that they had missed the Ferry. Oh well, I thought, but such is life. I was sad to see the disappointed faces of these passengers who could not board this boat, but I was sure that there would be another boat tomorrow. And then, hopefully, they wouldn't miss it again. I felt unusually optimistic on this trip. I guess, that was a good thing - only time could tell, and oh the way it did!

I stayed on the top deck for at least another hour, enjoying the panoramic view across Manila Bay. I could see the Makati skyline in the hazy distance, with its tall skyscrapers. And I could say, with full confidence, that it was the most beautiful scene I had set eyes on so far. The tall buildings and huge billboards complemented the clear blue sky all too well. I didn't want to move my eyes away from this view. I didn't want to miss anything. Makati City is the business hub of Manila, where banks, telephone companies, airlines, and many international businesses had their main offices. To think that such a "professional" city would mesmerize me this way, I believed there was nothing that could go wrong on this trip. I even felt like my decision of taking this trip was the best decision I had ever taken, in all my life. The smell of the ocean was a pleasant change from the stench of pollution that filled my lungs for the past three days in Manila. Looking around, I noticed some of the other passengers who were just as excited for the trip ahead as I was, and I spent some time talking to them. As I expected, they were a friendly bunch too.

Time passed by quickly as I talked to these friendly passengers, who were maybe also enjoying the view like me. When I was not talking to them, I would be looking around, either toward the scenery outside or to find something just as beautiful inside the Ferry. I also did not notice any other foreigners on the boat. It was now time to say my goodbyes to my new Filipino acquaintances, and it was a warm farewell. How all natives I came across with were so polite and friendly to me was beyond me. But I was not complaining. I, then, found my way back inside the Ferry and my eyes landed on a bar. Being a little thirsty from the excessive MSG in the food, it seemed like a good idea to sample an ice-cold San Miguel beer. So, I went inside and ordered a beer.

Looking around I saw that many passengers were enjoying this part of the boat and I decided to join them. As I was sitting alone and drinking my beer, some people approached me to make friendly conversation. And the next thing I knew, I was talking to three boys and a girl at the bar. Since I was feeling very happy and my mood was too upbeat, I bought all of the young boys and the girl some beers as well. The beers were not expensive and my gesture was much appreciated by my newfound young friends. My day was only getting better and better!

I have to be completely honest; over time, I felt attracted to the young girl that was sitting beside me and I started flirting with her, even more so after the boys announced with smiles that she was single. I felt like I had hit a jackpot. The girl was pretty and seemed educated, or at least she spoke in perfect English. That is why it was easy to make conversation with her. What's more, it seemed that she was also flirting with me, so it was all nice and happy fun. I mean, coincidently, I was also single and free now. Then, to my surprise, the group of three boys and this young, pretty girl suddenly said that they had to go and sing now. And on they went to the stage, starting to sing and play their instruments. Obviously, they were the Ferry Band. They were such a talented group of young individuals but it did not surprise me as, over time, I had come to realize that this country was full of very talented musicians and singers. The band played rock and roll songs, followed by a few slow love songs to give a mellow touch to the bar ambiance. I was totally enjoying the entertainment.

After their performance ended, they joined me again for a few more drinks. I could again enjoy my flirting with the young female singer now. However, knowing the Philippine culture, I stayed respectful and did not touch her in any way. There were also hundreds of eyes looking at my every move, and the fact that I did not want to make the girl feel uncomfortable. She had already given me her phone number, written clearly with her name, on a small piece of paper earlier. She was giving me positive signals and gestures, so I thought it was okay to play my chances with her. And then, maybe, time would come when we would be alone - as she seemed happy and very interested in me as I was to her. Then, after two more drinks, we parted our ways and I promised to be back for the night's performance. After all, the real fun in bars is always at night!

Back in my room, I was pleased to find that the champagne was cold. So, it seemed no better time like the present to enjoy this magnificent drink. I had to drink the champagne from a teacup since there was no glass to be found in my room, but I didn't mind. The Moet champagne tasted like the sweetest thing that a mouth could taste, and gave me an enjoyable feeling. I was looking out the window of my cabin at the ocean and sipping my drink slowly. Everything felt surreal at this moment. The ocean was passing by the cabin window, and the sight of the passing water gave an image as if it was all a mirage.

This moment in time was as tranquil as I could ever have believed possible. The sound and view of the ocean waves, a comfortable room, and the sweetest thing I have ever tasted that was touching my lips and pleasing my palate. I wanted this moment to go on forever. What a nice feeling it was, being as free as a bird and no one to bother me. Was this a dream? Well, I was not sure. But if it was, I did not want to wake up. This life was as good as it could get. I was just flowing with the current and found myself mesmerized yet again. How nice it would be to live this kind of life, where each passing hour seemed full of a feeling that the unknown ahead would be good.

Before I knew it, the bottle of Moet had become empty. It was good timing since, at the same time, the dinner announcement echoed through the room. The words were in both English and Tagalog, so it would be convenient for foreigners to understand - even though I was the only one on this boat. I spontaneously proceeded to the dining room and again, I was not disappointed with the food. I savored the deliciousness with utter contentment. After my dinner was consumed and was now settling in my stomach, I went for a brief walk on the top deck once again, where I could breathe the fresh sea air. It almost felt like some kind of drug, making me unable to pull away from it. I guess fresh air in this country was a rare commodity. I wanted to enjoy it as long as I could.

Soon after, as a little more time had passed, the sun started setting. It was giving a great show, as the sun sank into the ocean on the horizon. I was watching the sea, lost in the percussion of waves as the orange rays started filling up the ocean. Seeing the sun disappear down the waters, I felt a strange kind of nostalgia and a feeling I cannot quite describe. But what I know is that it was nothing bad. As the rays and hues of orange got darker, and the sun disappeared quickly, darkness soon followed. As it got darker, I remembered that I had somewhere to go and a promise to meet. So, I hurriedly returned back to the bar, excited to see the band play again.

By the time I arrived, the band was already on the stage, singing and playing their instruments. So, I decided to find a table to settle in and had to sit alone for a while. It didn't matter as I was enjoying the music from the Happy 4, as I called them. Maybe they were not as good enough to be called the Fab 4 yet, but after the champagne, it sounded every bit as good. I signaled and sent a tentative wave to the band. Smiling, they waved back and seemed happy that I was back for their performance as I had promised. Or maybe, they were thinking, "Great! Some more drinks later!" Realistically, I think they were happy to see my smiling face. My smile was always there these days, no matter what I would be doing. I had lost it for a number of years, for many reasons. But now that I had none of these reasons with me, my smile was now back, stronger and more frequent than I could ever recall it to be.

Chapter 4

MEETING CHERRY.

As the band continued playing, I was sitting and looking across the room when I noticed a stunning young girl walk in. She looked a class above the others, which was perhaps more so because of the way she was dressed instead of her actual beauty. Not to say that she wasn't pretty looking at all! She was sitting with an older lady, which in time, I learned was her older sister. Whenever I looked over, they would be continuously looking at me and so, I gave them a tentative wave as I had to the band. I knew that there was a girl I had shown interest in before, whose number I still had in my pocket, but it was not like we were committed to each other already. I could not keep my eyes away from this new beauty that I had found; though, in retrospect, I shouldn't even have waved at this girl. They kept waving me over to join them, so I eventually did. There was no reason for me not to.

In all honesty, I was feeling a little guilty as I had already made a play for the singer of the band. She was even watching me, and as I approached the other girl and her sister, she looked a little angry - as if she was already my girlfriend! We had only made some casual conversation and flirted around, so it wasn't anything serious. Ignoring her, and my guilt, I introduced myself to the young lady and her sister. She said her name was Cherry and her sister was Edylin. Both of them looked pretty, but my eyes and mind had already been captured by Cherry. From the first moment we had met, she knew what to do to keep me in the palms of her hand. She said she had just arrived from Japan and was going to Cebu, from where she would go on to Bohol. Bohol was the place she was originally from, as her mother lived there in Tagbilaran City. I shared my plans with her, which only included enjoying this Ferry trip and then finding other things to enjoy in Cebu. I guessed she would be one of these things that I had wanted to enjoy on this trip.

As time passed, I went back to the bar to buy the girls a few drinks. Then, I noticed the singer girl approaching me at the bar where I was buying the drinks. She was a very jealous and angry girl and looked at me with daggers in her eyes. I should have known what was coming at me, but it wasn't really a big deal in hindsight. When she saw me, she rushed towards me and started to raise her voice at me, using all kinds of bad words that she knew. I remember hearing words like "Bigaon" and "Babaero", which I later learned meant someone that had many lovers or someone who was a total flirt, a womanizer. The boys in her band noticed the commotion and hurriedly dragged her away before things got out of hand. So, I was relieved. I mean, I did understand that she was disappointed, but I felt like I did not deserve the anger that she bestowed upon me. Her words were not nice to hear at all. How could she go from this sweet, polite girl to a raging woman? After all, I was free and single and was only being friendly to people. Yes, maybe a little friendlier to girls. The only thing I was guilty of was happiness. All in all, this is how life is, and most people would not feel anything. But for me, being as soft-hearted as ever, felt like I had done something wrong. Though, of course, it was not the case in reality. The singer was way out of line to be jealous and angry at me like that. She didn't have to yell at me in front of so many people.

Feeling a little shaken up, I just had to put it behind me and put a smile back on my face. I couldn't just ruin my trip by taking such a trivial moment to heart and being sad about it. So, I gathered my composure and walked back to the table where Cherry and her sister were sitting, with our drinks in my hands. I had hoped Cherry and her sister did not witness my little drama, but even if they did, there was no mention of it when I returned. As we continued chatting up and gulping down glasses over glasses of drinks, I was starting to feel a little drunk. And it did not take long before I was holding this temptress named Cherry. Little did I know this would one day prove to be a very bad decision that would bite me hard. Maybe it was my karma, I will never know. But at that very moment, I felt like I was at the top of the world. With a drink in one hand and this temptress in my arm, there was nothing more I had wanted at the time.

By this time, the ferry passengers were taking turns singing, like it was now karaoke time with the band. Cherry, my newfound sweetheart, or so it seemed to be becoming this way, was still seated beside me watching the show. In future reflection, I came to realize that I was very drunk and was taken by a gifted liar and actress. I am sure I was not the first or the last, victim of this girl. As we talked about the performance that was going on, Cherry casually mentioned that she was a good singer. So, I being drunk and all in her control, passed the waiter a note with 100 pesos inside and voila! it was now Cherry's turn to sing. She sang this song called My Heart Will Go On in perfect harmony, and I could see that the girl singer in the band was not impressed. Maybe she was still angry and jealous that I had chosen Cherry over her. But to the young singers' credit, she was professional and they all smiled and clapped for her. As for me, it made me feel stupidly proud of this Philippine girl who worked in Japan.

Cherry and I continued to drink alone as, by this time, her sister had returned to her cabin. We drank until about 11pm and there was no sign of us stopping or leaving each other anytime soon. Though we did stop drinking in the end, we could both hardly walk straight. After all, I had been drinking for close to twelve hours. In my drunken state, I invited Cherry to my room. We both stumbled and staggered to my room totally intoxicated. Surprisingly, Cherry was not shy at all when I invited her for the night. Obviously, I was not the first man she had been with. Once inside my room I closed the door behind us, the first thing this girl did was unzip my pants and put my erection in her mouth. My first reaction was, wow! This girl knew more tricks than Linda Lovelace from Deep Throat, which is a famous porn movie from the 60's. Cherry was a very naughty girl and just as energetic and enthusiastic. She stayed in my bed until morning. My life with this devil was now beginning and I had no idea at the time that this was a bad decision.

Morning came far too quickly, and I was awoken with a loud announcement that said we had arrived in Cebu. Also, once again, the deafening horn was sounding, doing a good job of damaging the eardrums of all passengers. Before I could have time to even think, I was leaving the boat, still feeling the effects of over-drinking the night before. So, slowly, I was walking down the steps to the shore, dodging the porters coming onto the boat hoping to get some income from carrying the bags for passengers who needed assistance. They looked at me and looked at my girl, and never offered to help me. Maybe they thought that I had no money, judging from my old suitcase and the simple clothes that I was wearing. Nevertheless, it didn't matter as I didn't need help from them anyway. I was just holding this old bag and this girl I was too happy to be with.

Finally, after the slow descent had ended, we were now standing on the arrival port of Cebu. I was searching for transportation with Cherry and her sister Edylin. There were so many taxi drivers in my face, looking for a job to drive passengers to their next destination. It was total chaos and, even though the charges were double or maybe even triple what the original cost should be, I chose a driver and his price and we were all now walking to his taxi. The taxi had to park about 100 meters from the boat, so we all walked in the stifling heat which was made even hotter by the reflection of the sun off the concrete walkway. It was almost similar to the burning sensation I felt when I spilled the coffee on my hand, except that I was now feeling it on all of my body. I had "Maraming Pawis", or many sweats in English, dripping from my body. I guess the alcohol was now leaving my body. So, before long, and gallons of sweat later, we were in the car and I was on my way in this taxi to Plantation Bay. Cherry and her sister were also with me in the taxi, though I did not remember the night before when I had invited them to the Plantation Bay Resort for the day.

They were leaving for Bohol at 5pm, so we all decided to enjoy the remaining time together as much as we could. First, we went to this paradise resort swimming pool. We all swam in this resort swimming pool, which had to be seen to be believed. It was maybe the biggest swimming pool I had ever seen and dipped in. I was enjoying the swim and the fresh water in this huge pool when Cherry nudged me. She had the same naughty look in her eyes and I understood her signals. Following the swim, she once again took me to the bathroom and showed me some more tricks before it was time for her to leave. I noticed that this girl looked a little prettier with a big smile glowing from her pleased face. She simply wiped her mouth and got up, saying that it was now time for her and her sister to leave. Needless to say, I quite enjoyed the farewell gift from Cherry and was unknowingly looking forward to more. So, I waved goodbye to Cherry as she was leaving with her sister, and out of nowhere, I said, "See you in four days in Bohol!" I had no idea why I even promised to meet her in Bohol and visit her after my Plantation Bay holiday.

It was not part of my plans for this trip; but there I was, looking at this girl who was too pretty and too clever as I promised to get her back by following her to where she was going. It seemed that this girl already knew how to control me. And me, having nothing better to do and having no pressing schedule to run by, decided to stay in her control and be swayed by her tricks that were too good to be true. It sounded like a good idea to me at that time.

Chapter 5

PLANTATION BAY STAY.

I did not know how I slept! I woke up very festive like a bird in the springtime enchanting with joy and peace. It was a great night's sleep on a bed that felt like it was made for an Eastern King. I opened my eyes heavily like a newborn baby who first opened his eyes to the world. After resting for five more minutes in bed, I decided to get up and take advantage of this beautiful morning. The herald of the morning breezes gave me the greatest feeling. The greatest that I faced overall - to withdraw the dark mantle over my joyful heart. To fade all this away to silence allowing this shining morning and let my little bird flying again freely, singing new songs of braver freedom. I caressed all these feelings with my current emotion. I then had a magnificent breakfast which also seemed like it was made for a king! What a relief to sip a morning tea with the sweetest smell filling all the atmosphere! Although it's a fully healthy breakfast. I did not eat that much; I think because my heart was in total contentment.

Sometimes you feel you need eternal silence and relaxation, so now! I had three more days of relaxing, enjoying, and reflecting here in Plantation Bay. I sat on my sofa with the soft breeze murmuring with the atmosphere - then I remembered the girl who I had been emailing on the internet before I left Australia. I had known her sister before who was now married and living in California USA. She was the one who gave her sister my email address. I did not know where this idea came from - just suddenly I decided to text her. Without any hesitation, I sent a sweet message. I wondered if I did the right thing or not? Whilst I had been wondering, I got a response from this young girl very fast that I did not expect! I guess it was something reciprocal! She was happy and very surprised that I did text her, as I read a beautiful positive response which made me actually happy and wondered if she had been waiting for my text. I had plenty of time on my hands, so this was a good opportunity to spend some time together. I created all the scenarios in my mind before her response - only after I got her response that she agreed to visit me, I felt happier and played out many scenarios in my mind.

After a good breakfast and resting on my sofa, as my heart was in a good mood, I went for some exercise in the resort gym. I had to stay in shape, after all. I started with cardio - only then all alcohol in my body started getting out - after only five minutes I was like running under the rains, I felt so much energy, as my body started being light again and fresh. Though it was really hard work, I survived my workout. Then, I anxiously waited for the young girl that I had invited. I was all ready, and curious to meet her especially now I was feeling good after my torturous workout.

The girl I was going to meet was an 18-year-old student, who I had enjoyed chatting with through internet emails - as she did respond very quickly with a big curiosity I think or just her young blood sparkling to get to know more people and get more experiences. I just enjoyed the conversation, that's all for me, on the other hand, I was just in a good mood. A good mood to get to know someone new maybe! or just to have fun! We all need a person to spend time with, or just to talk with from time to time. Her name was Joanne. I know when you hear this name you will imagine maybe a French girl wearing a black dress and living with her glamour. Or perhaps an American girl living a poetry life like in an American movie. It was just Joanne, a simple girl from the Philippines, as like other Filipina girls. Now perhaps you get the vision of how Joanne looks. As I had been waiting for her arrival, I rang her up to inquire about her whereabouts. She told me that she was on her way and would be here in an hour - well, after four hours, she arrived.

I learned quickly that this was the way it is in the Philippines. Time has no real meaning or importance; it is called "Manyana Time". A Filipino will say that they are on their way when actually they are not. It's a common thing, which I later learned. In other words, this is just an expression that means I will be there "Mamaya" in Tagalog, which means the same as "later". So, there I was, just patiently waiting for this mysterious young girl to arrive. I slowly sipped my hot sweet bitter coffee, I spent some time talking to the friendly barista at the resort coffee shop, as I enjoyed the conversation and the vibes that he gave, he proudly taught me a little more of the local language which I was eager to learn.

All of a sudden, there was a loud noise of a motorbike that disrupted my Tagalog lesson. In the distance, there was a vision of a young girl arriving at the front of the resort aboard a "Habal-Habal" which is a small motorbike that is a fast and cheap mode of transport. Many thoughts were flashing very fast in my mind that I could not believe Joanne had arrived. I immediately recognized her but what shocked me was that she was wearing a school dress! She also wore two white ribbons in her hair and was carrying some school books in her arms. Why she chose to dress that way remained a mystery. I glanced at her, hoping she was not confused in some way and expected me to tutor her!

She gave me two kisses on my cheek like she was kissing her daddy when she was going back to school! I touched her hair softly - then with a smile on my face I said " Hello Joanne, you came very quick! " - in a sarcastic way. This is how it goes in the Philippines. You should have an absurd response to each situation. If you do not do that you will end up as a foolish person. With her sparkling eyes like a small candy which is about to fade away giving this little light in her dark eyes, she said "There was a lot of traffic!". I did not believe her anyway, because in the Philippines if you have an appointment, you should go out two hours before your appointment as traffic is part of their normal life. Anyway! We walked through the entrance of the resort front door; people noticed this young girl.

One of the front desk ladies in reception at the resort started asking me a lot of questions, particularly about the girl. I found these questions quite invasive and immediately shut her words down, though of course, I did it in a nice way by showing her the ID of Joanne showing she was eighteen years of age. I had no reason to tell the inquisitive lady anything else; after all, I did not know this lady so I felt I did not deserve her judgment. Two of the younger girls at the reception desk seemed very shy at the aggressive nature of the older lady's questioning methods. Many other people in the lobby seemed intrigued and uncomfortable too. From what I could see and tell, the stares from the other staff and other guests were both that of curiosity and disapproval. I did not care about any of them, their views, or their stares. I mean, that was to be expected. Ignoring everyone, I invited Joanne to my room and once in the room, the first thing I did was order food for her with room service.

It did not take so much time for the food that I had ordered to arrive. I noticed the waiter's expressions and once again felt the discomfort directed towards us. He must have thought that Joanne was my daughter, judging from his face which showed surprise. A little tip seemed to change his whole-body language to total approval. Then, Joanne turned towards the food and began to eat like a hungry child that had never eaten such foods in her life. Eating wouldn't even be the right word for it, she practically devoured everything! As for me, I was just sitting and watching her eat with excitement building in my mind. Oh! It was not because of how Joanne the mysterious student ate her food, but because of my own very vivid imagination. I was imagining myself eating her while, in reality, she ate the delicious food that was so courteously delivered to her.

This young, happy girl had a big smile on her face all day, her existence was very soft, without feeling any pressure in the air. I hate that kind of pressure that some people make, it just makes me feel very anxious. However, Joanne proved to be good company for me. After eating, she silently worked on her studies while I kept myself busy with a little of my own business. The quiet and peaceful atmosphere made me feel comfortable and good, even though both of us were indulged in our separate activities. When the night fell and it was starting to get darker, I decided to run a bath for my young guest. She was not shy at all and used the toilet without closing the door. She seemed excited to enter the large bathtub with many fragrant bubbles. What came next surprised me even more than when I saw her arrive in a school dress!

She took off her clothes very slowly with the soft lights reflecting from her skin and just like Chopin playing some nocturnes in the middle of a storm. She showed off her tiny beautiful body with aesthetic details of her as her hair was touching her skin very softly only then she lifted her hair to get in the bath. Whereas I was enjoying this show, Joanne invited me to join in with her in the bath. My response was rather slow, all because of the sudden shock I felt and also my indecisiveness about it being okay or not to join her. I hesitated about her invitation and thought for a while. Well, what harm could it do? I thought to myself and concluded that I should accept this invitation. I quickly undressed and climbed into the warm bath filled with many fragrant bubbles, and also a young and pretty girl.

Being with a girl totally naked and in the bath together, it was only natural for me to have an erection. Though I had to hide it with a face washer, which I was using to wash this young girl's back. She said nothing, even she felt something, as hard as a piece of wood, that was rubbing on her back. She knew I was very excited and felt it also, but why she kept quiet about it, I didn't know. I bathed my pretty young school girlfriend for at least half an hour. After that, she returned the favor by washing me too.

All in all, our bath together went great, and room service was next on the agenda. Tonight, we would eat our dinner on the balcony, looking over the magnificent swimming pool that still had people swimming in. It was refreshing, only seeing them enjoy the pool even though it was well into the night. The room service attendant soon arrived with our dinner and seemed now to approve of what he saw and another little tip was welcomed with a warm thank you. Soon it was bedtime, Joanne and I watched a movie on the cable TV channel called HBO before we both fell into a deep sleep. Though we slept together kissing and being sweet, I did not go any further than that. Even though I could smell her wetness and realized that she wanted something more, I controlled myself. Not in my mind though, as I considered licking all of her juice and imagining how it would taste. In the end, though, I didn't do it.

Well! you can call me old-fashioned or just stupid, but I felt like she was still a child even she was of legal age, as

I'm not Humbert Humbert. Even though she said she was eighteen, I was still not convinced. It was obvious that this very young girl was a huge temptation or "Tukso" in Tagalog to me, but I was glad that I only slept with her and did nothing else. It was amazing to me how strong and stable my self-control was!

Morning came too quickly. With the same energy as the previous morning, it merely seemed like I had only closed my eyes for a few minutes, and it was morning. Joanne had to leave today, but first I insisted she must have breakfast before leaving. Once again, the stares from other guests and the staff were long and frequent.

I took no notice and said nothing, but for a split second, I wondered what was going on in their mind. Well, who cares, right? I then, bid my sweet little guest farewell and gave her a little "Baon" or money to help her with her needs.

After another relaxing day at the resort, I caught the afternoon hotel free shuttle bus to Cebu City for a change of scenery. I decided to shop around a little before I ended up in a place called Illusions - a bar I had frequented the last time I was in Cebu. Young students would come to this bar looking for foreigners that would reward them for their company. After the night with Joanne, I needed some relief. After last night I was now feeling hornier than a stallion servicing a field of mares the whole morning. It may be hard to believe, but very true. So, I entered, anxious and excited to see what I could see inside.

In the bar, I glimpsed at a cute girl looking at me, I headed up with virility, only after two or three words, I befriended this pretty young girl and wasted no time inviting her to come home with me to Plantation Bay Resort. Yes! She agreed without any hesitation to accompany me for the night. With a lot of words that have no meaning and giggles, we got out from the bar, without noticing how we did take the taxi. All I remember was we were in a taxi on our way to the resort. I was very discreet in the taxi. However, once we were walking to my room, I started holding her soft hands and gave little slow kisses to my newfound beautiful friend. When we arrived in my room, I was taken back by what stood in front of me. My friend from the previous day named Joanne was sitting inside my room! I had no idea how she was able to get inside, maybe I left the door unlocked was my only thought.

Suddenly, I felt bad and was very shy. I found myself in an embarrassing situation. I did not know what to do to explain or to discover what was going on here. I only stood up very surprised and gazed at Joanne, I felt the pressure that I hate was filling the atmosphere, the girl who gave the comfortable vibe now puts me in a very anxious position. The new girl that I had picked up from the bar was also trying to understand the situation - then in a very fast manner, I came up with an idea. I said without any vibration in my tone and without any changing of my manner to my new found which had the name Sandra that she was the niece of my friend and I had brought her with me because I wanted to show her the resort. Joanne acted okay and it seemed like she believed me. As for me, I knew the whole time she was well aware that Sandra was a naughty girl and there was no doubt that I had other plans for her.

Recognizing the heavy tension in the air and feeling the need to break this awkwardness, I invited both girls to have some food and we all went straight to the resort restaurant. I ordered some delicious dishes for the three of us and watched the two girls eat too well, maybe not knowing where their next food would come from. Then, Joanne suddenly said that she had to go home and continue some studying, leaving me alone with the naughty girl, Sandra. I soon realized that Joanne was a good sport and wanted to make no trouble or interruption to our plans, which seemed to be clear to her at this point. That was why she left us alone, to not intervene in our plans tonight. It was a big relief for me, as I had already had a taste of Filipina drama on the Super Ferry. Thankfully, that did not happen again.

The night went amazing with this naughty girl Sandra, who was the supposed niece of my friend. Both of us were so horny, also she was so passionate in bed, whilst I had been grabbing her waist strongly with both my hands and hearing her moaning with her sweaty hair over her body. You can imagine how Sandra was naughty the whole night, as she was a fresh girl with a long neck and face like an egg very clear as her lips were shaped perfectly. We had a perfectly enjoyable time together. I was beginning to enjoy this country and the warmth of the beautiful Filipina girls that lived here. I did understand them because, in this country, these girls needed to survive as best as they could - since their opportunities were very limited.

The next morning, we had breakfast in the room as I think if the lady at reception saw me with a different girl, she might have had a total meltdown. Also, it was an image that I did not want to portray to other guests that saw me the day before. I then gave her a goodbye kiss. I said farewell to Sandra and wished her the best for her future. The rest of my day was just spent relaxing, swimming, and getting healthy with a great massage. I wanted to make as much of this day as possible as it would be my fourth and last day to stay here. Tomorrow, I planned to visit Bohol and meet up with the girl named Cherry, the girl that I had met on the Super Ferry. So, this day was a quiet relaxing day at this magnificent resort named Plantation Bay.

I had a great sleep and enjoyed my bed alone. And then morning was here, it was time for me to check out and go to the terminal of the fast boat called the Super Cat. It would be about a forty-five-minute taxi trip away from the resort to begin my next adventure, which was a trip to Bohol.

Chapter 6

BOHOL TRIP.

Anything could now happen in this life, I enjoyed my stay at this beautiful resort with the beams of sun and the delicious breakfast every cheerful morning, I felt like I was in eternal peace. I did not imagine anything later; except I was very excited about my new adventure. My heart was like the thunder before the rain, I was only hearing the voice and waiting for what this trip would bring to me. Even a man if he took a long time relaxing under the sun, enjoying the small details of this life, whereas he is lying in the bed enjoying life with the peaceful harmony like Johann Strauss II melodies, or just like butterflies dancing with flowers in springtime, he feels very happy. Only then he hears a voice coming from nowhere telling him that he should take a new challenge.

Here I am now boarding a hydrofoil-styled boat called the Super Cat, with a two-hour trip to Tagbilaran City Bohol ahead of me. As I boarded, I noticed that the sea waters were bubbling from the exhaust of the boat, and soon, the strong smell of diesel fumes filled all of the passengers' lungs. My journey for today was now starting. Once I was on board, the boat suddenly became deafeningly silent as the boat's air-conditioning dried the sweat from my body, making me feel human again. By this point, I was getting used to traveling by boat and enjoyed it too.

While I was seated, with my lungs full of diesel fumes, I just kept in my place gazing at the people and their reaction. Most of the passengers were relaxed and silent. As for me I was very excited and my heart full of adrenaline like coffee running your heart beats like a wild rabbit, why does it run this fast? I still do not know, but I know the rabbits run when they feel a hazard come close to them or sense danger. I remained in my seat very relaxed and did not sense any danger or mishap on the trip. Then all of sudden the big TV screen at the front of the boat started flashing, as it started giving a safety demonstration, explaining the emergency procedures in case of a mishap on our trip. This was then followed by a very deep prayer for all passengers to feel safe that God was now protecting us on our voyage. After the demonstration and the prayers were completed, they started playing a drama Tagalog movie on the big screen. I was all ready for the entertainment when I noticed a man - or so I thought, sitting next to me. He was wearing a dress and smiling but instead of being rude and telling him that I preferred women, I just closed my eyes and pretended to be sleeping. And just like that, with my eyes closed and body relaxed, I arrived at my destination with the trip being smooth and without any problems.

After my peaceful sleep onboard, I was now refreshed for what was to come in Bohol. These sorts of sleeps make you learn how to stop caring about other people's lives and focus on yourself. I arrived at my destination without any headache, I was in a very peaceful mood following the boat trip. I got off the boat then I breathed very deeply a new air to perhaps change my thought patterns after the boat ride or just to feel that I am in a new place and I should adapt to it. The soft breeze was touching my face, I smiled then I glimpsed, Cherry was waiting for me at the pier. She was looking provocative, with high heeled shoes, tight jeans, and an equally tight top like she was trying to show her features in a bad manner, which can only make you feel curious for what was ahead. She was passionate about fashion, she looked good and was dressed in a very alternative way. Her lips with bright red lipstick were glistening in the afternoon sun. From afar, I was thinking that this girl was a prostitute before I got closer and recognized that it was, in fact, Cherry. She did look like a slut wearing her skin-tight clothes. Anyway, after we both recognized each other, I gave her a warm greeting with many hugs and kisses. Her perfume was very strong and its intense smell similar to the diesel fumes of the Super Cat. I did not know if my lungs were full of diesel, or just her perfume was making me light headed.

Before I knew it, we had hired a tricycle, which is a 125CC motorbike with a sidecar attached. At that time, it was the only means of transportation from the Pier. So, we had no other option except to take the tricycle. We then squeezed into the tricycle with my bag tied securely to the roof of this small vehicle, then we were off to a place that Cherry had wanted to stay at. It was called the Bohol Beach Club, a secluded resort on Panglao Island. It was very clean with a large blue majorelle swimming pool and the green landscape surrounded with coconut trees on all the sides that merged with the beauty of the blue clear sky and the sun decorated it, like a big pumpkin. There was also a sandy beach at the front of the resort and a verandah where you can sit and enjoy the heavenly ambiance of this place. After we both checked in the resort, we were given cold towels to freshen up. Not only that, they even handed us a free drink as a welcome. I was impressed at their service, but then again, that was to be expected when I was paying $100 American dollars for a night here. I guess this is the type of service that you deserve to receive, with that much cost. Nevertheless, I had a feeling that I was going to enjoy this day.

We were now settling into our room and I was given another deep throat experience from Cherry as a welcome. After my treat, we both were now sitting comfortably in the room with the soft breeze moving the curtains very slowly. I was wearing a very light shirt, I felt the summer breeze was dancing with my emotions, especially the emotion of nostalgia and missing something. I got up, then I opened the doors to the verandah very wide to get the sea view. We could look over the beach from our room's verandah, and the view was perfect to be paired up with some glasses of champagne. So, we started savoring the last two bottles of Moet Champagne that I had reserved for a special occasion. Well, this moment seemed as special as any to me. All was good at Bohol Beach Club, and I was in bliss and satisfied. With great service, a great view, and some bottles of champagne, there was nothing else that could make this moment feel any better.

As the day turned to night, Cherry and I were both exuberant. Now, this devilish girl again showed how much fun she could be. She was good at what she did. And when she did it, she did it in a very good way. Cherry was truly experienced in what she was doing. This devil girl was playing very hard, very hot like the burning sun, her tricks, could make you see the stars on a bright day. She could sometimes be unexpectedly exciting and I would find myself thinking that her tricks were out of this world. Cherry was a happy-go-lucky girl and we both enjoyed drinking together. I was enjoying myself with her and it seemed that her company made my trip somewhat more exciting. I was glad that I took this trip with her, that I chose to spend my time with her instead of any other girl - in the middle of these feelings I thought about my life! I got the feeling that it always felt like the storm before the rain or the silence before the thunder! I was very confused about this feeling of silence that this trip had given me. Time with Cherry would prove this to be a false feeling.

On the next day, we wanted a change and checked out of the resort. Even though it was a nice place, it was too isolated. We decided to go back to Tagbilaran City and stay at a place called Bohol Tropics instead. So, before lunch, we were checked out and were on our way to the next destination. Once again, we had to travel by tricycle and went forward to our next port of call.

Arriving at Bohol Tropics, I noticed that it was a native hotel-style resort. It was located on the edge of the water and I liked this new location better, as I always loved the simple cozy places that afford this calmness and the feeling of being home. Bohol Tropics was full of native styled huts and palm trees. Where the palm trees exist, I existed! At night, we went for a tranquil dinner as we had a good talk - then Cherry and I made a plan for a trip to Chocolate Hills. I was very fascinated about this idea, and I was always excited to see new places to discover the small details of each place and talk to the native people. I was Ok with this plan especially for a beautiful amazing place that I only heard about in a documentary. We planned to visit the Chocolate Hills which is a unique group of hills that are near a town called Carmen. So, with a few texts and a few phone calls, everything seemed to be organized for our trip tomorrow. Though all was going well, I had no idea what to expect in this ever-changing day-by-day world I was now living in.

Since both of us were now excited for our day of touring the island of Bohol, we got up early in the morning and were ready to set out by 8am. The hired van, or jeepney as it was called, arrived on time and we were ready for our day's trip. However, to my surprise, there were already an extra ten people sitting inside - that I did not recall inviting, all ready to go with us. Two of these extra passengers moved onto the roof to make room for us. I was happy these two boys gave us their seats as looking at them on the roof of the jeepney did make me think it's better for them up there than me. "Oh well, the more the Merrier", I said to myself. Though I wasn't expecting them, I didn't mind it either. We then loaded up the jeepney with plenty of snacks, ice, and four cases of San Miguel Beer. At the last stop, we also picked up a whole roasted pig to add to the delicious collection. The pig was cooked over charcoal which the Filipinos called "Lechon". We loaded this precious final addition carefully in the back of the jeepney for good measure. All was going well.

We had only just departed on the jeepney and just a few minutes into the ride, and all of the passengers were already drinking beer and eating snacks that we had loaded inside. The loud radio and the singing voices of Filipinos soon filled the air, as did our excitement. With how outgoing and upbeat these people were, you couldn't even think about getting bored on this trip. I could not help but smile at their liveliness. And before long, a cold beer was placed in my hand with the cap removed. I noticed that one of the passengers used his teeth to break the bottle cap open; that explained the number of broken teeth in his mouth.

The ambiance was very lit! They did actually afford a very cheerful vibe to our trip, with very crazy things, and singing out loud with the wind coming from all the sides, as the cold beer was matching the sunny weather, I felt my life was flourishing like a wild poppy flower in the wheat fields. I did keep a smile on my face the whole trip, sometimes singing and sometimes laughing and sometimes reminiscing the good memories which are flashing by very fast with each second that makes me feel very thrilled and excited. Our first stop was at a beach on Panglao Island, where we all swam, laughed, and enjoyed the local alcohol called "Tuba". Oh, that drink was playing in my veins, giving me the running wildly in my feelings like it was a combination of dopamine and adrenaline - It was a fermented coconut drink that delivered a kick with every sip I took in.

The next thing I knew, my head had started to spin after this drink as I stripped down to my undies and still managed to swim in the ocean with all the other passengers. It was very refreshing and I felt as if all of my energy had been refilled when before my swim it was the other way around. So, after our refreshing swim, we were soon back on our jeepney and onto our next stop. The next stop was about forty minutes far - the Loboc River. Once again, several bottles of beers were flowing and the singing was getting louder and louder. At this point, I was enjoying it so much that I even sang along!

The sun was kissing our skin and my sunglasses were giving a clear vision of nature and also the colour of the beer was matching with almost the skin colour of the natives. The toothless one, he kept serving the cold beer like we had no limits. I was really enjoying the trip with my very simple companions - this is what we called true happiness. It is when you enjoy the little things and appreciate every second of it, enjoying the sun, the sky, the oceans.

We arrived at our next stop with the same energy. I was amazed at the new scene. I could see miniature squirrels or little rat-like creatures in a little forest on the banks of the river. These cute little creatures were known as "Tarsiers", and they proved to be a great addition to the already beautiful view of the forest and river. One of the main features of these cute little things called Tarsiers was their huge eyes. These eyes did not move, but they could see from side to side by turning their heads 180 degrees in both directions! These creatures were unique to this part of the Philippines only, and at one stage, there were about eight of them crawling on my chest and shoulders. Luckily, they did not bite.

After my play with the little creatures, it was now time to eat the roasted pig or Lechon that we had brought along on the jeepney. There were no plates, knives, or spoons as we had neglected to bring them, and yet, we were still able to eat the Lechon using only our hands. This was nothing new to these people and they simply said "Kamayan" which means eating with the hands. Nobody seemed to mind as we all continued to devour the pig, pretty sure looking like pigs ourselves until there were only bones left on the animal's carcass. In the end, we all agreed that the Lechon was delicious. Now, it was time to hit the road again, for the highlight of the trip - the famous Chocolate Hills.

Another forty minutes passed, and we arrived at our destination. I immediately got off the jeepney and there I was, looking up at a gigantic set of stairs that seemed to ascend on and on towards the sky. It reminded me of the tale of Jack and the Beanstalk, and I hoped that no giant would appear and eat me at the top! Logically, of course, this was not going to happen. So, without hesitating, I started climbing and passed hundreds of steps before finally reaching the top. I was breathing heavily and my heart rate had elevated as well, but looking out from this high position, all of my exhaustion went away.

My breath was taken away, not only from the steep climb but from the amazing sight right in front of my eyes. I was looking into the distance and it was a breath stealer. The view left me speechless - I could see hundreds of little, big, and round hill formations as far as my eyes could see. Some hills were brown, some green, but all of them looked truly amazing. I had been to so many different land formations on this planet, but this one was so unique. I had never seen anything like this before, and I doubted if I would ever be able to see a better sight than this again.

The legend of the Chocolate Hills says that the hills came from two giants who started a war by throwing boulders at each other. This continued for days but the boulders were left to form these hills that we can now view and enjoy. This might sound unbelievable, but a part of me believed that it was all true. This view looked too good to be all-natural; there had to be a story behind it. At the end of the day, whether this legend was true or not didn't matter. We all got to enjoy it and that's all that mattered.

After a long gaze across the Chocolate Hills, I watched the sun begin to descend. It was now time to climb back down. As all of us were intoxicated from a full day's drinking, we slowly stepped down the steps. Once we were finally back on the ground, totally relieved none of us fell and broke our necks, we then all went back to the jeepney and headed back to Tagbilaran City. It was a day well spent, a trip well enjoyed, and snacks well devoured. This day, to me, will always remain memorable. It was a fun and adventurous time all in one. From morning to night, we had enjoyed the beautiful waters, forest, hills, little creatures, and beers. Although it was a little (or honestly, a lot) expensive, it was all worth it in the end. Another thing I was sure about was that all the passengers would also come to remember this day for years, as it's not every day that a Santa Claus comes to town.

After this long day came to an end, I will always keep this memorable trip in my mind with every small detail of it, especially the passengers who were with us, the cold beer, the song that we sang and also the magnificent view of the Chocolate Hills. I felt that I returned to nature on this trip. I found myself through the small details of humankind that gave me fulfillment. I would now have a good night's sleep like an exhausted human. Tomorrow, I would be on the move again, with an early 6am Super Cat boat ride to Cebu and a flight on to Manila.

Chapter 7

MANILA HOTEL.

The morning sun arrived again as usual with its warm beams and beautiful heat and I did not want to get up from my bed especially as Cherry had her body lying over me. For a while, I wanted to remain in bed for the whole day, but I carried my body to have a hot shower and to get fresh to be ready for the next trip. We woke up very early around 5am to catch the boat that would be leaving the Tagbilaran City Pier in an hour at 6am. We packed very slowly because we were utterly tired but for me, I did not mind! I was very excited on each trip, you can find me with the same energy with the same ambiance, even if I'm just going to Manila. We left heading toward Manila full of memories of all these beautiful places that we did visit. Before long, both of us were back onto the Super Cat and on our way to Cebu departing Bohol after a crazy tour, which turned out great. I definitely planned to return here one day to explore more of this unique island. But, for now, all good things had to come to an end. It was time to go to Manila.

On arrival at the Cebu Pier, I felt something weighing lightly on my shoulders. I do not know if It was that I was missing Bohol or just the effects of the Chocolate Hills tour. Perhaps because I am carrying new memories. We gathered our bags automatically and found a taxi to take us to Cebu Mactan Airport. It was where our Philippine Airlines flight would leave for Manila, and it left about two hours later than the appointed time. Cherry was also accompanying me to Manila as she would have her dance classes there. So, I had to make a seven-day booking in the Manila Hotel, which was an old but famous hotel in the Philippines. One of the reasons for its fame was that General Macarthur had stayed there during the second world war and this General one day said "Old soldiers never die; they just fade away" and I think inside me there was a strong soldier who never died, who never faded away. He remained tough, strong, and brave. A lot of strength was needed to hold them feelings towards the world, towards a specific person.

Everything was flashing with the unforgettable trip which is now a souvenir that I will always remember. All the destinations, I was merely having a peaceful mind and the effects of the trip still in my mind with all the details. Only a voice woke me up from my daydream of my memories! The voice was making the call that we will be landing in few minutes at Manila Airport. Even though the conditions were clear and no drama, the plane seemed to bump a lot during our flight. Maybe it was the age of the plane or some other reason, I would never know. After a rough flight from Cebu, thankfully, we arrived in one piece - which was the only thing I cared about. The taxi ride from the domestic airport was long and slow due to heavy traffic on the road which was nothing new in Manila. In this country, it seemed that anyone who could afford a down payment on a car would immediately get one. The narrow roads, bad driving, and no courtesy also did not help the traffic problem. Horns from cars were continuously tooting and were piercing the ears of every passerby.

The jeepneys, which were large and long vehicles painted in various bright colours, have a bench-like seat that was fixed on each side of the rear section. They were the most attractive moving objects on the road. They would almost always be playing loud music as the way things worked was the louder and more attractive the jeepney looked, the more passengers they will attract. This is the main public transport for locals and would continually stop in the middle of roads to pick passengers up or drop them off. There were no designated stops for them, so it caused a lot of traffic disturbance. All in all, the traffic situation in this city was nothing less than chaotic.

We finally arrived at the Manila Hotel, once I entered the hotel, I was amazed at the history and feel of this sophisticated hotel with a view of the magnificent bay, and a combination of extraordinary beauty and warm service. Manila Hotel was not only a hotel, but it was also etched in history especially visited also by the Beatles which caused a diplomatic incident. The decorations and memorabilia from the floor to the ceiling were the best I had ever seen anywhere in the world. The staff were also dressed for the part, to complement the decorations. In pure white pants and shirts for boys with white caps, and the girls were dressed in traditional Philippine dress which was befitting to the historical feel and setting. We checked into this amazing hotel, but I felt overwhelmed that I had the chance to see and sleep under the ceiling of this hotel.

The main reason why I was in Manila was that Cherry had to come here to do her dance training for a week at Quezon City. She was getting ready for her return trip to Japan, where she worked as an entertainer in a club. I do not know what kind of work this is but I have a big intuitive background and these kinds of work bring more troubles in life. However, I wanted only to live free with no drama, no tragedy. I am not a Greek God that can bear everything. As for me, I only have a heart full of pure emotions. Emotions that I wanted to invest in someone. Someone who appreciates love, passion, affection, and tolerance. My heart was open-handed and fragile.

At night, Cherry confessed to me that her ex-boyfriend was a drug addict and was starting to send her threats via text messages. I started wondering, how long had this been going on and why did he have Cherry's number in the first place. I did not ask her any of that though. Then, she asked me if I could hire a friend of hers to act as her bodyguard for the week. I was the one who had to pay for the hire. I agreed - though, I was a bit hesitant. The whole scenario wasn't making sense to me. Still, I agreed to Cherry's request after she shed a few fake tears so I will stupidly believe her. It was all because of her acting prowess that I lost my sense of rationality and believed every word she said. Or maybe it was the impersonations of Linda Lovelace from Deep Throat. Well, whatever the reason, I agreed and was falling into her trap.

The next day, early in the morning, we met the so-called bodyguard of Cherry at the hotel foyer. He was a very handsome young boy, who looked about twenty-five years of age and was named Jojo. The very first thing he said very confidently, was asking if I would like him to kill Cherry's ex-boyfriend. I was shocked at his suggestion at first, but soon that shock turned into anger. Why would I have someone that I did not know murder Cherry's ex-boyfriend? I was not a murderer, and would never be. The young boy was extremely overconfident with his body language, liking to that of a person who controlled the world with intimidation. As soon as he saw and noticed the anger on my face, he quickly took back his offer and did not pursue it any longer. He looked at me with anger in his eyes and I started to have a really bad feeling about the whole setup.

After some questioning from Jojo, we came to an agreement that he would pick Cherry up from the hotel and escort her to her dance classes every day, bringing her back to the hotel at night. I agreed to pay him 2000 pesos per day, which roughly converted to $60 Australian dollars at that time. From what I learned over the years of knowing this devilish girl, I would confidently say that each day, these two would have bought a popular drug named Shabu with the money I gave and probably booked a cheap hotel somewhere to spend the day together. In hindsight, I highly doubt that there was any dance class at all. I guess it was all a made-up story to get money and freedom. At the time, I was too innocent for these Philippine lies and tricks. I genuinely thought that Jojo was only helping me protect my girl.

Coming back to the current scenario, Cherry who played the great role of the crocodile with tears in her eyes, and the bodyguard left the hotel together. I invited a friend named Gary to visit me at the Manila Hotel. He was staying at a place near Mabini Street called the Iseya Hotel. It was a hangout for old Australians who liked to drink and pick up girls. When he arrived, we sat by the hotel pool all day and enjoyed some drinks together. At that time, Gary was pretty down on his luck so I agreed to set up a business when we would be back in Australia. I wanted to help him get back on his feet. After all, it was my nature - helping people and being kind to them at every chance possible. In my life and experiences, I learned that this was a stupid way to be. Did anyone really appreciate my kindness? Human nature isn't as good as I wanted to believe it was; most people I helped did not appreciate me or my help, but even laughed behind my back. But, at the moment, I still had a long way to go before I would learn this reality.

The day seemed to speed up and pass by quickly. At about 7pm, Cherry and her bodyguard arrived and before I knew it, the boy had left quickly. Though, he did say he would be back tomorrow. Because of this setup, I had all day to do whatever I wanted while Cherry would be at her supposed dance classes. But in my heart, there were echoes telling something else, telling me that Persephone girl would take my life from my hands, my freedom, my values. Cherry has something in her eyes showing all the tricks and the devilish deeds that she is willing to do - Me! I was blind, I was not capable of seeing obviously how this girl would mess up everything. I merely fell into a careless manner or just I was having an absent mind and a blind heart, that would cost me a lot. I knew from my past experiences dealing with many different kinds of people, but I kept taking the ride with all the masks that this devil girl was continually wearing.

So, the next day, I walked up to Rizal Park which was named after the Filipino hero, Jose Rizal. This hero was incidentally buried in this 60-hectare significant urban park. The locals called it Luneta Park which was its original name. This park is located in Ermita, about a ten-minute walk from the hotel. I walked around in this park for a few hours and then laid in the sun on the grassy lawns for a while. It was so vast and quiet that this park was giving me the feeling like it was a Persian garden where a nightingale was singing with the rhythm of my heart, enjoying the soft breeze dancing with the leaves wildly, I felt I traveled away with my mind to merge with the blue clear sky. I ended up napping under one of the shady trees, which were vast and plentiful in this magnificent park.

The day went very quickly in a beautiful harmony without caring too much about the physical life. I then went to my hotel happily. Suddenly I came up with a plan for the next day. The plan was to organize a tour. On the third day, I was ready to go for the tour that I organized. This time, a van came to pick me up from the hotel at 8am and drove me to the ferry for a thirty minutes boat ride to Corregidor Island. Other passengers beside me were also maybe going for an all-day tour to Corregidor Island, which was situated at the entrance of Manila Bay. This was where General Macarthur was held up and the island was fortified to defend the city, until the Japanese forces, in 1942, forced the famous General to leave. The US forces reoccupied the island in 1945. The tour ended up being informative and opened my eyes about the past, as the tour guide showed us all the ruins of the bombed buildings, old artillery, guns, and cannons, with the highlight going through the bomb shelters and tunnels which were also used as hospitals for the wounded in World War 2.

As for my last day, I spent it alone, checking out Intramuros – the Wall City that the Spanish fortified dating back to 1571. It was only a fifteen-minute-long walk from the hotel. On my way, I noticed a lot of young students around the area and saw that there were many colleges in the vicinity. I had to be strong and keep control of myself to not fall into the temptation of these pretty and friendly Filipinas. It was going all good, and I enjoyed my touring days as I learned more and more about Manila and its history. So, this was how my week went: Cherry would leave early in the morning with her bodyguard while I explored the city when she was away. Just like that, six days passed by in a flash.

It was now Sunday and the day for Cherry to leave for Japan and go back to work. Her 21st birthday was coming up on March 30, so I told her I would visit her in Japan at a City called Saga. I promised to spend time with her on her birthday. So, for now, we bid each other goodbye or "Paalam" as the locals say, until we would meet again. I did not go to the airport with her but instead, hired a hotel car to take her to the airport. After all, it was a four-hour round trip and I also felt that it was not necessary to accompany her and endure the stressful drive. So, the hotel car was a practical and safe way to go.

Soon after seeing her off, I was beginning to miss my young devil but, at the same time, felt like I was free after being with her for almost two weeks. Then, there I was, alone in the Manila Hotel for my last night. To make the last day count, I decided to visit the Tap Bar on the ground level and found a seat for myself at the bar. There was a great traditional band playing, which consisted of a piano player, a bass guitarist, and some guitar players. All the instruments were acoustic and gave a smooth feel and sound. The vocalist looked like an elegant lady wearing a stunning black gown and high heels. Her hair and makeup were groomed to perfection. This lady, I would say, was about thirty years of age yet had an amazing professional voice. It seemed that she had a lot of singing lessons when she was younger, judging from her extraordinary voice and vocal skills.

After the first set of songs, the elegant lady took a seat on the other side of the bar from me. I sent her a tentative wave and said "Hello! You are a very good singer". She instantly replied "Thankyou" with a happy smile on her face. I then asked the barman to offer her a drink to which she happily accepted. And the next thing I knew, she was sipping on a cocktail. I was thinking more on the lines of a beer but, of course, a girl of her prestige was not cheap. It looked like she was a little nervous, judging from how quickly she finished her drink. Little did she know that I was much more nervous than her and thought maybe, she was a little out of my class. I went on to offer her another drink and this time, she then came over and sat beside me. The barman then served her another cocktail, which I realized was called a Pina Colada - the one that they mention in the song of the early 80's with the same name.

The elegant lady barely had time to finish her second drink, and after some small talk, she was back on stage to continue singing like a songbird. In about forty-minutes, she sang eight songs and then again, took a seat beside me. She seemed pleased as another cocktail was waiting for her. When I smiled at the other band members, they frowned at me in response while giving a disgusted look on their faces. I confirmed from the elegant lady that she was single and none of her band members had any personal relationship with her. I wondered why they gave me that look, then again maybe they were just some serious musicians but, by this time, I did not care, and it sure seemed that neither did she. We were both holding hands, and before she went for her next set of songs, I gave her a little kiss on the cheek to be sweet.

I did notice that this set was not as good as the previous two, and her songbird voice was not reaching the high notes as comfortably as before. The band members also looked agitated at this point. After this set, she came back to drink her fifth pina colada cocktail, but who was counting? This time, we were even holding each other and getting as close as ever. Before I knew it, we were kissing each other as though we were the only two in the whole room.

The band was now on stage for the fourth and last set, and my singer friend went up after being called twice. So, with one last kiss, she staggered toward the stage. At this point, her hair was becoming a little messy and her makeup was in urgent need of a touch-up. But this elegant lady was on stage, trying her best to sing as well as she could while holding the microphone stand in a way that seemed she would fall if she let go. After only four songs, the band surrendered with embarrassment as my newfound friend had become very drunk. Her singing, - to be polite, was a little out of key.

We were back together. And once again, she was sitting on her chair and drinking - all while being touched discreetly by a very naughty man, - me. Then, I ordered some food and one more drink, asking them to deliver it all to my room. Although we never got around to drinking the last drink or eating any of the food. However, we did end up having a passionate night together. The next morning, I took her for breakfast, and she was wearing her dark sunglasses. As we left the room, we noticed the food and two drinks at the front door. The lady in sunglasses was so shy now, obviously due to last night's treat. Noticing her shyness, I apologized but she said I didn't need to as it was the most fun, she had in years. After having breakfast, I bid her farewell by giving her a sweet kiss goodbye.

Chapter 8

THAILAND TRIP.

I daresay I had a wonderful night with the girl that enlightened my spirit with her attitude. Besides her shyness she was keen the whole night that we spent together. Regardless, the time went very fast. I went back to my room with a big smile on my face - perhaps because my heart was full of enthusiasm for the next trip or just the impact of last night. Then I lay on my bed gazing at the ceiling, imagining about what this life would bring to me. I needed to get ready for my flight. I should leave for the airport in two-hours to catch my flight that was leaving at 1pm. I got up and began packing my bag. I also had plans to visit Pattaya or Sin City as it was known. Once again, I felt the rush of excitement in my body as I prepared for my next trip. Maybe because I had not been to Thailand since 1993.

Whilst I had been packing my bag, my mind reminisced about my last experience when I was in Bangkok. It wasn't a good memory. It was my first trip overseas when I visited Bangkok. And all you know when it is your first trip, we get confused, we get very anxious like a deer in the middle of the wild. Who just stood up in the middle waiting or just looking? My last trip seemed to have stolen the sweetness of my travelling. Travelling is very good for our fantasy. It makes our body and our heart work well. You need to have travel experience to which brings you more joy. Last trip I had a lack of travel experience. I was robbed and forced to sleep on the streets for a week with no money. This time, I had experience and a little more money, also a credit card. I was determined to make new memories in the City of Temples.

Soon, I was on board a Philippine Airlines 747. The take-off was smooth, and so was the flight. After two and a half hours from Manila, we were touching down at Bangkok Don Mueang International Airport. My arrival was late afternoon on a Sunday. I was disillusioned to see a long lineup at immigration, but all I could do was to be patient and wait for my turn. Eventually, I got my reward for my calmness and patience, which was a stamp in my passport that stated I could remain in the Kingdom of Thailand for thirty days. With a smile of excitement on my face, I then collected my bag which was floating around the carousel, waiting for me. And within a few minutes, I was in a yellow taxi on my way to Patpong.

The taxi driver dropped me off in the middle of Patpong, and without too much trouble, I was able to find a cheap but clean hotel called the Happy Hotel. I really liked the name because I was feeling like a happy man myself. Then, after dropping off my bag quickly, I proceeded to explore and have a few drinks in some of the girly bars in this noisy notorious place. I was propositioned for sex from so many girls who were looking for some money, but I refrained from the temptation and ended up in a Thai Restaurant at the back of Patpong. My stomach was grumbling like an angry bear, and I felt like I could eat up everything on the menu. I ordered a Pad Thai which is an addictive traditional dish that is made of rice noodles with a sweet-savory-sour sauce scattered with crushed peanuts and gives you a true taste of Thai cuisine.

When the food was placed in front of me, I wasted no second and started eating at that very moment. I almost even chewed my fingers off along with the food! It was very delicious food and I was hungry. Sometimes when I feel peace in a place the first thing that comes to me is a good appetite. I would say this is a peaceful but also a hustle and bustle city. Besides the tasty food, the waitress who took my order was about twenty years of age, was very friendly to me. Her beautiful smile was so attractive, and her body language was very smooth like a flower dancing with the wind. I kept gazing at her for a while trying to read her name on the badge with my wide-opened eyes, as I glimpsed at her slim body in the uniform of the restaurant. I said in my mind "This girl is nice! more than my food". So, I couldn't hold myself back and asked her if she would like to meet me after her work. She never replied but I told her my hotel name. Then, I paid the bill and left a small tip before walking back to my little hotel room to get some sleep.

After a few hours in a deep sleep like the fallen prince, I heard a noise coming from far away. However, when I was woken up slowly with this noise, it was only the room phone ringing at about 2am. The call was from the reception downstairs, informing me that I had visitors. I was a little surprised, but not really shocked - even if I was not sure who it could be, though I was hoping it would be that young girl from the restaurant. After all, no one else knew that I was staying here. So, after the call, I quickly dressed and proceeded downstairs. To my delight, it was the pretty young, smiling girl from the restaurant! She was now dressed in a beautiful pink dress and was smiling shyly. Together with her, was an older lady and I recognized her as she was also from the restaurant. This lady was encouraging the young girl to stay with me for the night, and even though she was shy, she agreed as she wanted to stay with me.

I was very tired but also happy. My heart was like in a field of lavender dancing, enjoying the magnificence of the muses. And while my heart is filled with joy, I start being generous and friendly more than limits. So, I said "Kap Khun Krap" meaning thank you in Thai, to the security guard and the older lady. I also gave them 200 Baht each, as a goodwill gesture. Now, this pretty young girl from the restaurant was my girl, at least for now. She stayed with me for the night, and I could describe what happened but some things are better left to the imagination. What I will say with all honesty though, is that my tongue was quite sore the next day.

After two days in Patpong, which I spent relaxing and checking many markets they have here in this well-known tourist area. Every night before sundown, the Thai workers would erect the light steel constructed stalls and stock them with everything that is branded from Louis Vuitton bags to Polo shirts. But they were all copies of the original branded products. The workers would then return at about 2am and pull everything down, ready for cars to use for the day. To my amazement, this was the pattern of events in Patpong Markets 365 days of the year.

Now, it was time to leave this place too. So, I booked four nights in Pattaya with a local travel agency and before I knew it, I was on a bus to explore this new place. I had heard many reports that this town was known as Sin City. On arrival, I noticed my hotel was at the north end of the town and was shaped like a large boat. It was also appropriately named the A-1 Royal Cruise Hotel, a very nice 3-star hotel. Pattaya was a noisy bussing town, full of massage parlors and girly bars which catered to the large number of tourists - which was everything I had expected of this place.

The first thing after I arrived at the hotel, I went for a swim in the small but refreshing hotel pool. I also talked to some of the guests from many different countries for some time before I set off to explore once again and see what trouble I could find here. Pattaya had a long beachfront walk and all along the beachfront were prostitutes of all shapes, sizes, and ages - even men dressed as women. Ignoring them, I walked for at least one hour before feeling like drinking a cold beer. So, I stopped at the front of a clean-looking drinking bar during my walk. Soon after, I befriended a waitress who said her name was Toohey. It was also a name for an Australian beer at the time and maybe that was one of the reasons that I started liking this girl. As the coincidence of the smallest details of the city was meant to be for a reason! I took the flash again. We drank a few beers together and I was pleased just how simple she was. Also, another thing I liked was that she only drank beer, not cocktails or hard liquor.

After these drinks, I then asked Toohey nicely to be my tour guide for the four days while I was staying here. After all, I did not know the place so well and her local knowledge would be a big help, especially because this girl spoke good English as most Thai people did not speak English well. Toohey went and talked to her boss, who was a tall and sexy lady in her early 30's. She asked for four days off and her boss then came over to talk to me. I guess she wanted to meet me and see if I was a normal guy before allowing that to happen. She proceeded to introduce herself as Wendy and the first thing she said to me was that she was married to an English man who was also the owner of this bar. Then, she explained that I had to pay a bar fine, which was how things worked here in Pattaya.

I agreed and surprisingly, it was quite cheap. Only 400 Baht per day. So, I paid this lady 1600 Baht while Toohey gathered her things and put them in a little bag. Then, off we were on our way to my hotel. Maybe those things in her bag were all her worldly possessions. After arriving at the hotel, the security guard insisted on holding her ID which Toohey agreed to give. She then explained to me that this was the normal way things work and it was to protect the hotel guests from theft or something worse.

After spending the night together and having had a nice conversation where we told some old stories of our past. It was a simple night but very quiet and comfortable. I did not feel any pressure or any kind of heaviness. I love those beautiful nights. Just a peaceful nice talk with maybe a few beers or not and enjoy the company and keep everything simple. We woke up early the next day as we had planned to visit the crocodile farm. Actually, it was something that I wanted to see. Soon, a van came to pick us up and dropped us after a thirty-minute ride. The crocodile farm looked interesting and they also had a show where this crazy Thai man put his head deep inside the mouth of a crocodile. I could never understand why he did this as this prehistoric creature could easily bite his head off if its jaws closed. The sight made me shudder but I let it be.

The man then explained that they had a flood last month and over two hundred crocodiles had escaped. I was just about to gasp at the number of crocodiles they lost, but he genuinely proceeded to tell us not to worry as they had already recaptured one-hundred-and-eighty of them. I could not help but think about where the other twenty crocodiles would be. Then, I had my photo taken with some lions, rode the elephant, and generally just enjoyed the day.

The following days were spent having steams, saunas, and massages at one of the local health spas. Though Pattaya had many spas to choose from, all of them were pretty cheap. We chose the one that had two large elephant statues at the entrance. Every night, I and Toohey would then have dinner at a restaurant that served sukiyaki named MK's. The food was magnificent, delicious, and very healthy. Almost all of the menu consisted of healthy foods in this restaurant. It was also really popular with the local Thai people, which I guessed was because it was very inexpensive. While walking around town, I also visited a travel agency to purchase a four-day package tour to Ho Chi Minh City Vietnam, which was previously known as Saigon. Knowing that it was my last night, we decided to watch a live sex show which was actually a freak show with young girls spitting ping pong balls from their pussies, and bananas and even firing darts at a dartboard. The finale was to watch a young girl having sex with a Thai man in front of the amazed crowd.

The next morning, time had now come to leave. So, I bid farewell to Pattaya and also to my tour guide, Toohey. I also left her a good reward for her kindness and hospitality. She was a good lady and I felt that my experience here was much better with her guidance. We both had become close after only four days but there were no tears or any kind of drama when I was leaving. She just smiled and told me to enjoy Vietnam. I then realized that Thai girls were very hard-hearted.

After about a two-hour van ride, I was back at Don Mueang Airport and before long, I would be boarding my short flight with Thai Airways to Saigon Vietnam.

Chapter 9

SAIGON.

Although Don Mueang Airport was crowded, I calmly and patiently survived the long check-in line. The airline crew were very friendly with a good sense of warm hospitality. Youthful enthusiasm flew through my veins just like a wild river that made me excited to see this city. After about an hour and twenty minutes, my short flight with Thai Airways from Bangkok which was "Smooth as Silk" was on its final descent. Before I knew it, the plane was touching down in Saigon which is the largest city that has an irrepressible spirit, it is also considered as the heart of Vietnam beating day and night. Vietnam had only been reopened for tourists, perhaps, fifteen years earlier after the war that ended in 1975. So, with almost a century of colonialism and brutal conflict I kept in mind the recent history, I imagined and expected that the country wouldn't be so modern. I guess my opinion was formed when I noticed how old the airport looked upon arrival.

The tour package I purchased in Pattaya also included a hotel transfer in the deal. Once again, after going through the same procedures of customs and immigration, I then collected my bag and I was finally outside the terminal. Once I was outside the airport, I saw a smiling Vietnamese man with black sunglasses and also had a moustache who was holding up a handwritten sign with my name written on it. I recognized my name very fast, as the man holding the sign also notice me quickly like we did know each other before. This was a big relief to me, as I didn't have to go to the trouble of finding my transport, especially in this country with chaotic taxis and lack of organization. I really had placed a lot of trust in the Pattaya Travel Agency. I also felt relieved that I had arrived. When I approached the man holding up my name, he seemed very happy or maybe relieved as he welcomed me with a big smile on his face that made his eyes smile too. Though he did look surprised with lifting his eyebrows when I told him I was all alone on this trip, but he said nothing.

After greeting each other with a firm handshake, he grabbed my bag and escorted me to his taxi which was clean and smelt like new, everything was cool and simple with no worries at all. I thought that he treated this taxi like it was his wife, with special care and it had a good odour filling all the inside of the taxi which had polished leather seats. Before long, we were on our way to town. I was pleasantly surprised when we pulled up outside my hotel. The hotel I was dropped off at looked very nice with an elegancy which you can see in every part of this hotel and everything was well organized, also it had an exquisite bar and restaurant at the rooftop with an amazing view. The Rex Hotel was the name and was located in the middle of Red Square, as they called the area outside the hotel. Around Red Square were red communist flags with yellow stars and pictures of Ho Chi Minh, the leader of the country, drawn on banners - which was naturally the reason for the name of the city that was changed from Saigon to, of course, Ho Chi Minh City.

Coincidently, the day I arrived in the city was also Chinese New Year. So, it made me feel even more excited as there would be a lot of celebrations for the Year of the Dragon tonight. It was also relieving that there was no war here now, and felt like the future has arrived in this city. So, all in all,

I had many reasons to celebrate. First, I walked up to the city center and noticed that many locals were also out and about. Crossing the road was going to be almost impossible, as hundreds or maybe even thousands of small motorbikes were six and seven abreast flowing endlessly through the chaotic streets beeping their horns in perfect harmony - or, at least, that is what they thought. I had no choice but to cross the road. So, I did, finding myself dodging against the motorbikes on the way which also caused me to twist my knee which gave me a sharp pain under my knee cap. This sharp pain did not feel good. It even stayed with me for the next four days and I was limping all through this time. I didn't know, until a week later, that I had damaged my knee pretty badly and would need surgery to repair the damage.

After the motorbikes and my knee incident, I reached the other side of the busy road and it felt like I had just gone through a marathon, even though the boulevard crossing seemed endless. Such was the relief I felt, to have conquered the motorbike gauntlet. I even threw my arms up and cheered like I had won the event. Then, I looked around and found a street-chic bar, which seemed to be full of friendly people. So naturally, that was where I headed. After finding a comfortable seat at the open-air bar, I sat down and rested my knee while I sipped on a cold and refreshing local beer. Soon, I began enjoying the amazing fireworks that were brightening the dark sky above. The young locals were cheering loudly every time one of the fireworks exploded in the sky above. These simple people were extremely happy, and it was a nice feeling throughout the City of Saigon.

The fireworks show went on for what seemed like an eternity, but realistically, maybe, for an hour. I was then sitting and minding my own business when I was offered a ride home from a pretty and friendly Vietnamese girl. She had a small motorbike and since I did not feel like walking because of my injured knee, I happily accepted her offer. I noticed that this girl did not look pure Vietnamese and was obviously half American. She was very attractive - so much so that maybe, in another life, if she was born lucky, she could have been an actress or at least a model. Well, she seemed happy just where she was for now.

I told her my hotel name and sat on the back of her bike. Then, she handed me a helmet which, seeing the way the locals rode, I immediately put it on my head. Whether she did not understand me, or whatever reason it was that she took me to a small boarding house, I never knew! She had her own rented room there. Maybe I was too naive for my own good, as I later realized that she was a prostitute. Instead of being disrespectful and leaving right away, I went inside her room. It was a small room with a mattress on the floor and a very small bathroom. This girl, after I took some time to look at her, was a real beauty queen. She also had the body of a model with a tiny perfect waist and very long beautiful legs and delicious thighs like a fresh French creme. I kept looking very slowly at this beauty! I could not stop myself as I pinned her over the wall very gently and I began to kiss her sweet lips slowly like Debussy was playing on the piano, her lips were shaped like a heart and she was a flower without a heart. Then, she took me in the shower, which was an exaggeration as it was actually just a hose from a faucet protruding from the wall.

This girl washed me down well as the night smoke and my sweat needed to be washed from my body. I reciprocated and also washed the girl well, especially around her vital area. She moaned a little and seemed a little horny, but I was sure that she was nowhere near as horny as me. As we dried off, I started to kiss her again like I was eating one of those delicious dishes when I was on my Thailand trip. I laid her gently on the bed. Then, I started to lick the juice, which was so wet and tasty. By this time, I was so hard from her taste and quickly climbed on top of her, inserting myself deep inside. We made love and enjoyed pleasuring each other for the next two hours.

I then sadly realized that it was time to leave. So, both of us slowly got dressed and soon were back on the motorbike. She dropped me at the front of my hotel and I gave her a few more kisses before waving her goodbye. I did ask her to stay with me for the night but she said that local girls were not allowed to stay in hotels with foreigners unless they were checked in on arrival. All through that night, I thought of that beautiful sexual experience with the girl who had movie-star looks. I kept reminiscing our time spent together until I finally fell into a deep sleep.

The next day, I woke up with a lot of energy like a King who won a great battle. I rewarded myself with a healthy breakfast - enjoying the happy morning, although in a while I felt like I was in a movie, it is not reality. I smiled from the bottom of my heart - Then I said to myself "Well if it is a movie then I am a great Director!" I finished my breakfast and then drank some hot black tea. After breakfast I went to Singh Café which is a place that tourists and backpackers stayed. It was similar to Khaosan Road in Bangkok. It was a mass of drinking bars, restaurants, and travel agents with tour operators. There, I was able to purchase a tour to explore the Cu Chi Tunnels and relics of the Vietnam War, which I booked for the next day.

The tour operator arrived on time the next morning. It was going to be about a two-hour van ride from the city. During the ride, we stopped halfway to visit a jewelry shop. There, we saw how the jewelry was made and some people even bought some of the items for sale. As for me, I refrained as I didn't have anyone I could give it to. The only girl that came to my mind was the one from the other night, but to find her again would be like finding a needle in a haystack. After some time, we arrived at our actual destination. There were old tanks and small tunnels in which the Viet Cong soldiers lived inside, hiding from the enemy. That was also from where they would ambush the French and American soldiers during the war that nearly destroyed this country from 1955 to 1975. This was a big mysterious war, with a lot of historical stories, with a lot of innocent people who got engaged in this war perhaps because of poverty or because of honor. And most of them hadn't known the main reason why they got involved in this brutal war.

The tour was then completed with a short propaganda movie that they played during this period to brainwash the people and motivate them to fight the evil enemy. All in all, I enjoyed the day and it was all well worth the experience. I arrived at my hotel from my interesting and informative trip very tired. I headed up directly to my room and slept well. Tomorrow was going to be my last day in Saigon or Ho Chi Minh City.

The next morning, I was approached outside my hotel by a friendly old Vietnamese man with a rickshaw. He looked worn out, haggard, and sundried, and had a thin body. He looked about sixty years of age but maybe, he was only forty. So, after a small conversation, I hired him for the day to show me around. I had taken an instant liking to this old man and we were acting as if we were old friends. Then, he took me to visit the war museum and a few other city tourist spots.

After some time going around the city, I suddenly started feeling guilty and offered the old man that I would be the horse for a while. He did not accept my request at first, but then, after some persuasion he allowed me to be the driver of the rickshaw sometimes. I then realized, being the driver, how hard it was pulling the rickshaw in the Vietnam heat, and my injured knee added more pain to it all. Still, it was a great day and my knee miraculously survived, even though I was wondering how much more damage I had inflicted on this painful major body joint.

My newfound friend, this old and simple Vietnamese man and I, were enjoying and laughing at each other's jokes. Before we knew it, the night fell. I invited my guide to join me for dinner as a parting gesture. He humbly accepted my invitation and we found a nice old-fashioned and French-styled restaurant to eat. It was by the Mekong River and we sat outside and ate well. We also sampled the house's special Escargot, which was a dish consisting of cooked and edible land snails. I enjoyed this fine dish and it was the first time that I had tried something as exquisite and delicious as this in my life.

We also savoured a few beers together and I could see how much he appreciated my company. I enjoyed the dinner and laughter even though our conversations were pretty limited. And then, it was time to say our goodbyes to each other. I then gave him a friendly hug and handed him a good reward for his day's services and guidance. My Saigon trip had been memorable and I knew that one day, I would return to Vietnam and explore more of this city. Feeling tired now, I went back to my hotel room early to rest as tomorrow I had to fly back to Bangkok. From there, I would fly home via Manila to Brisbane Australia.

Chapter 10

KNEE OPERATION.

It was a long trip from Saigon via Bangkok and Manila that I felt for a moment that I will always live in this big plane and it seemed to me that this trip is endless. Although I was looking for something to entertain me, I ended up checking the time and the destination and looking at the tired faces which did not give me a sign to open a conversation with anyone. From time to time, I was smiling with the lady hostess in which she smiled back with a fake smile but at least she smiled. My body was feeling very heavy. I wanted to have a deep sleep and a hot shower when I arrived home. I wanted to keep myself a little bit away from adrenaline and focus on my life. With long patience and a tired body, I arrived in Australia with big relief in my chest that I am finally home. I had been away for so long and felt exhausted. However, in reflection, I was pretty content with what I had experienced in such a short period of time. I had visited so many places and met so many people that the past month felt like a whole year. I was feeling somewhat depressed to be back in Australia, or maybe it was just a feeling of reality taking hold of me. The past month, my life had been surreal and full of amazing experiences.

I did observe that even when I am at home, I missed the happiness and enjoyment that I felt in Asia. I miss the harmony of how people are very kind to each other, I miss the rhythm of chaotic busy streets and the neon lights of chic simple bars. I miss every detail of my trip, especially the good old Vietnamese man with his humble attitude to life, I miss all the friendly smiles, and Yes! I miss those fire nights that I was with the beautiful Asian girls. The girls had a lot to do with my feelings and I knew that. I closed my eyes and I let every detail of these amazing memories flow inside me like flashing pictures. I smiled with a heart full from those wonderful experiences. I breathed deep and I figured out that on the Gold Coast, no woman would be interested in me. They say Australia is the lucky country, and maybe it is, but I did not feel lucky to be home - I actually felt the opposite.

Here now in Australia and this time, I had many things to do before I would be able to leave again. So, I knew that the best thing I could do was to switch on and stay focused. So, I met up with my friend Gary, who I saw in the Philippines a few weeks earlier when I was staying at the Manila Hotel. He was really down on his luck. And being the soft and kind man that I am, I kept feeling sorry for him. I decided to start a business myself and give him half of the profits earned from there to get him out of the gutter. In all rationality, I must have been stupid as he had robbed me before, a few years earlier, and yet I wanted to help him. Why would this time be any different? I guess I was too kind to ignore his problems and do nothing; I couldn't live like that. So, I took the decision to start a business and worked really hard to set up a website, registered the business name, then printed all the stationery that would be needed for the business, and before long, the direct mail business was up and running.

Next on my list was going to the doctor. The pain in my knee from my Saigon trip had become unbearable at this point so I had no option but to go and see a doctor. Examining my injury, the doctor referred me to a knee specialist. Now, I knew that it was not a small injury and something much more serious was going on with my right knee. The specialist confirmed what I had been suspecting; I had a tear on the inside of my knee. It was so badly damaged that I needed surgery. I expedited the surgery and two weeks later, I was in the operating room where my painful knee was being repaired.

During the next three weeks following my knee operation, I was doing rehabilitation and it was really hard work. However, I knew that it was the only way that my knee could become manageable and hopefully, go back to normal. So, I kept up the rehabilitation work and never complained about the pain. I knew that I needed to endure it at this time. I planned to leave Australia again, once I was okay to travel and my knee was back to normal.

It was all like daydreaming, sitting in my home. All I heard was the noise of the last trip screaming inside my mind. I felt bored! All I wanted was for my knee to heal very quickly. Striving for the new trip to search for meaning, staying at home was killing my feelings. However, during all the time I had been in Australia, I kept in contact with my Philippine girl looking for good entertainment! The devil Cherry wasn't an innocent girl, she was surrounded by a fog which you cannot see through and even her words were like clouds very transparent sometimes and sometimes has no meaning! All I wanted is somewhere and someone to make me come down and to smile, something to make my life shining again.

Our talk was very smoothly flowing, sometimes with good endearment that shows a kind of lascivious feeling, otherwise, something was sparkling my heart but I still have no request. All of a sudden, this dangerous girl somehow convinced me to come to Japan and visit her in Saga. This town is a small city on the Southern Island of Japan called Kyushu. I remembered that it was her 21st birthday coming up and I had already promised to visit her on that date. It seemed that I had no choice but to go. I must say that I was easy to convince as I was looking for an excuse to have time away from my native country. Cherry, was also pushing me to come for a visit and I had no reason to not keep my promise.

Chapter 11

JAPAN TRIP.

Time passed by quickly, as my knee healed much faster than I expected. I now felt I became stronger than before. This made me feel happy and like the world started smiling at me again. Before I figured that out, I was onboard an Ansett plane to Osaka. Cherry had me in the palm of her hands and her power was controlling. After reaching Osaka I then had to change planes for Fukuoka. While waiting to transfer planes from Osaka to Fukuoka, I was amazed as about six young Japanese girls approached me and asked sweetly if I would take photos with them. They even bowed while they requested the photos. Of course, I felt privileged at that moment and agreed to the girls' request. Then, the girls took turns getting photos with me. The scent from these girls was worth the effort and Yes! I will admit, my mind did wander to the gutter during the photoshoot. I thought they did not see many Australians in Osaka at that time, so maybe that is why they wanted photos with me - I was a novelty to them. Or maybe, I was just handsome. Yes! that must have been the reason. It was all fun and then, the girls bowed again and thanked me for the photos. I told them that it was my pleasure but none of them spoke English. So, I simply said "Sayonara!" which is Japanese for goodbye and they giggled while we parted ways.

I left with an innocent smile on my face, to have this feeling of travelling, changing planes, waiting to check-in, and hearing all the noises of the airport. The adrenaline which was running wild in my veins mixed with dopamine made me very happy and excited, as I was smiling at everyone who I did meet like a child whose parents took him to a zoo. I was headed up to this marvelous country Japan with all the history, all the culture, and the good society. Without knowing how things had passed by, soon enough, I was boarding my next flight which was aboard a Japan Airlines plane. We were headed toward Fukuoka, the capital city of the Southern Island of Japan. The flight took three hours before I arrived in Fukuoka. On arrival, I then hired a taxi to my hotel in Saga and was charged 10,000 Yen for the ride, which at that time roughly equated to $150 Australian dollars. The ride was expensive but, no matter how much I haggled with the price, I had no other choice but to pay the price asked. The drive took about one hour from the airport to my hotel. Fortunately, and to my relief, I was dropped off at the correct location. Before, I had been a little concerned on the trip as the driver never spoke a word of English.

Upon arrival, I hastily checked into this small six-story building and dropped my bag off at my hotel room. It was by far the smallest hotel room I had ever seen in my life. In a hurry, I then exited the hotel to find the club where Cherry works. I also tried to get some directions from the front desk but again, no one there seemed to speak English. What made it a lot harder is that even all the signs there were written in Japanese. I had a small note in which I had the club's name written in English, but of course, it was of no help. So, off I trekked and started wandering the streets of Saga in the cold freezing night.

I did notice how quickly the time was moving and I desperately wanted to arrive at Cherry's club before the closing time. Therefore, I proceeded to check out every street, then eventually after a lot of walking I found the street that I was looking for. Now, I only needed to find the club that Cherry worked at. In this street, there is a lot of different kinds of colours of buildings. I found the building number and began climbing the steps, floor after floor of the five-story building, and checked the photos of the girls on each level. The building was full of clubs and finally, I found the club that my devil princess was working at by seeing her picture from the photos of the girls who were working there. Every club had displayed pictures of girls that worked there on the front wall. The pictures were reflected by the lights of the club that made each picture seem very enticing and Cherry in the picture was clearly like a doll running from a Hollywood movie. The picture of this little Cherry was very attractive to the eye. Something was about to tell the truth, but unfortunately, the picture was silent. Anyhow, I believe the reason was to lure likely customers such as myself inside. So, I was sure that this was the place.

I entered the club with a confident step to meet the devil woman named Cherry, as my eyes were gazing at each corner for everything flashing and giving the signal. The heat of the club changed the whole atmosphere that leads me to think that I should find her very quickly. Suddenly, I heard the word "Irasshaimase!" which means "Welcome" or "Please come in" in Japanese, as I later learned. I was immediately and eagerly escorted by a sexy Japanese girl who was bowing and had very thick makeup on. She smelled like a mixture of cheap floral fragrances, also she was wearing very high heels with a short dress. She seemed to me like she was also running from her past and she ended up working here. I created these stories with my mind to analyze very fast the rhythm of this mysterious club.

She took me and sat me at a table and I asked her with a half-smile and my eyes full of curiosity, but I did not show this curiosity. I was acting like a careless man without any discreteness or being introverted, as I acted like a customer with a gentle word I asked "Is someone named Cherry was working here?" She said "Yes" and soon, my devil girl Cherry appeared in front of me. She looked shocked as she saw me there. Just like the other lady, Cherry was also wearing a very short dress and high heels. And this time my vision was right. Cherry was like a doll running with a drama and tragedy. She wanted to be left alone but she never wanted to leave. She wanted to stay but she wanted a new life. She was swinging between two worlds as if she was walking on a very tiny wire that makes her not see life from another perspective. Cherry was this kind of these people who were stuck in their shitty things without noticing that they were sinking very deeply into it. She was playing with a big arrogance, with a big illusion, with a big dream that she is Del Rey from this little place. Though she looked more like a slut than the lady who seated me, she seemed very happy to join me.

The way it worked in these clubs was, you had to pay by the hour for the girls to join you. Drinks were served as an extra, but of course, no cuddling or kissing was allowed. So, I used complete discretion. I was then encouraged to buy a bottle of Hennessy XO Cognac which, even though the upfront charge was big, I agreed as they would hold it for me at the club. That meant I could drink it every time I visited, so I agreed because I knew that I would be coming here a lot over the next week. Inside, my every move was watched by all those who were in the club. I think that was because it was very rare to see an Australian in these parts of Japan. Or maybe it was just that they thought how stupid I was to come all this way just to see a girl. A girl who was a glorified prostitute which, at that time, I did not know. I wasn't a wise man. I was too kind and naïve for my own good. After all, this was my first time in Japan. I had heard the term "Japayuki" but never made the connection that this term described girls such as Cherry.

I had very little time with Cherry as she would only come every night to my hotel, mostly at 2am, to stay in my room. On this trip, my diet consisted of three meals a day - I ate from Lawson Station which was the Japanese equivalent to 7Eleven. I would only spend two hours per night at Cherry's club as it was rather expensive to table her. So, other times, I enjoyed frequenting some of the local karaoke clubs. They were a lot of fun as I drank and sang karaoke very badly with the locals. Luckily, no one seemed to mind or care. I came to discover that the Japanese were a very friendly, caring, and happy group of people. The week went quickly and I had a lot of fun with a lot of drinking. I also got to enjoy many saunas, hot baths and even did some sightseeing in the limited time available. Just like that, my week went far too fast but I had a memorable time.

I hardly had any quality time with Cherry on this visit. I knew that I would return here one day to meet her again. But for now, it was time to go home. I had to focus on my business in Australia and get back to the harsh and bitter reality for a while. I had my fair share of fun, singing with the local Japanese people and came to realize on this trip that they were genuine in every way, but now I had to get serious. So, I said my drama-filled farewells to Cherry and Japan, and soon I was back sitting on a plane heading back to Australia.

Chapter 12

MONTHS IN AUSTRALIA.

Japan, this old land, like the rising sun, always continued to rise with a combination of the old with the new, and the new with the future. With the beautiful energy of this country, the neon lights and the noise of the people make your soul intimidating. However, Japan has a specific soul dancing in a beautiful harmony that makes you fall in love without noticing. I did enjoy a great week of fun in Japan. Learning a lot and discovering the culture, meeting the people that were actually needed to lift my spirits, although I was a little bit careless about Cherry, I was very happy to be in Japan and spend so much time exploring, laughing, having fun to the fullest. The country was worthy to see even though it was a long-distance away. I felt refreshed again, as I was ready to start my own business. I went back to Australia because I perceived that it was time to get working and get busy. After that, I could go for more travel and maybe visit Cherry again sometime soon.

So, I landed in Australia and started getting into a serious work attitude. I now needed to push myself and try somehow to become focused. By the time I arrived, my property settlement had been finalized after the failure of my second marriage. That was a very expensive lesson that I had to learn. My marriage of two and a half years cost me dearly. No one would believe it, even I myself couldn't! I could talk about this marriage and expand on the expense but I had now moved on and cut my losses.

What is better than being a free man? A peaceful mind that I needed was now my first priority, I did not care about any other loss. The most important thing is I did not lose myself to please someone or to make someone happy who actually caused me pain and a lot of poison. I learned there is not much cheaper than a woman who does not have the sense of being a woman. I thought that I would find a shoulder that I can rely on but unfortunately, this shoulder let me down. I will now gather my strength and follow my new path in life which, even in my own mind, I doubted was the right one. Well at least, I was able to keep my biggest house that I proudly designed and built with my own hands back in 1999.

Up until the age of thirty-eight, my trade was a carpenter and that is how I was able to build my own house. As for now, I had a mortgage after my payout to Pamela. At least, I was free of my second wife, the demonic woman who was just a gold digger and an actress. Oh well! These are the lessons that we must learn in life. Stupidity will always cause problems. I now believed that I was at least ten percent smarter, because of this traumatic experience. However, as time passed, I realized that I had maybe become ten percent more stupid.

I was now living in my house and was trying to enjoy the beauty of the Gold Coast. After all, they say that this place is "Beautiful one day and perfect the next". One thing I can proudly say about the Gold Coast is that it has the best climate in the world. All this is true but only as long as you could live without the Asian lifestyle which also included young girls and the pleasures that they offer. Since I had no such opportunities here, I spent some of my time surfing on the golden beaches and enjoyed the warm waters that it was offering. However, most of my time was used up in building my business, working hard, and trying to make some money.

All during this time, I was also keeping in contact with the little devil Cherry who was still in Japan. Hardly a week went past without some sort of problem or drama that she would claim to be facing there. I had no idea if it all was true or not, though one thing that did concern me was when she said that she was being forced to take a drug called Shabu against her will. So, after dull months and hard work, it seemed like it was time that I needed to go to Japan and visit Cherry. I wanted to get her out of there as she kept painting a picture to me that looked pretty evident that she was trapped in a living hell. Being the soft-hearted and tender man that I was, I couldn't just ignore her or her problems. So, I planned to leave Australia as quickly as I could to go to Japan and rescue Cherry. I wanted to help this girl with her problems.

The following day on my morning beach walk to Surfers Paradise, I visited the Japan Tourist Bureau, where I was able to buy a one-week rail pass for my trip. I intended to fly to Tokyo and from there, I would catch a train to Fukuoka. So, I bought the pass in Australia, which was much cheaper compared to buying in Japan. After this I was now all organized to fly back to Japan and save my girl. I did have a strong feeling this was crazy but already I had made my decision to be with Cherry and did not count the costs. I think being in Australia and loneliness was affecting me and staying in my huge two-story house alone surely would eventually send me to the bridge ready to jump. I will be honest the words "There is no fool like an old fool" was taking up some of my thinking.

Chapter 13

JAPAN RETURN TRIP.

My mind was with Cherry in my every thought, she occupied my mind in a strange way that I could not resist. I allowed myself to get sucked slowly into this dark cave of her eyes. She was an abyss where all the demons chanted a song of hell. The hell was her heart controlling in many ways. I was just a little innocent child in front of this Japanese doll. I was then digging deeper into her underground. Underground built with flashes - flashes riding lies - lies riding black heart - then I rode these flashes not full of curiosity but because of my kindness. Kindness that would one day cause me a lot of hurts, a lot of wounds in my heart that cannot be healed. Her spells might cause me pain. Pain is very important to live; it makes you learn.

The clouds were passing by, and I was flying high in the Australian summer. Summer always makes your mind want to travel, want to have a journey, which this journey is unknown to your heart. I was now on a plane to Tokyo and after about nine hours in the sky, I landed at Narita Airport. Here, the customs and immigration were very tough on me, with the immigration officer asking me many questions that required precise and immediate answers. His uniform was like that of a Japanese wartime soldier and his face had a strict intimidating look. He even searched through the entire contents of my luggage, virtually checking every single thing that was in my suitcase. I wondered why they were so strict here? while my other trip went by without the trouble of such a thorough search. After the intense inspection, the man then bowed and said "Arigatou!", which is Japanese for "Thank you", and smiled. I smiled back and said, "Thank you, Sir!" It seemed that now we both respected each other in some unusual sort of respectful way.

I left the airport, and my mind was still confused about why I was intensely searched with tough instructions that customs just applied to me! I did not know why. However, I headed up to the exit to go out from this airport which gave me a different feeling than the last time I was in Japan. With my hand holding a ticket for a door-to-door bus service that I had bought in Australia, after a lot of looking around and searching outside Narita Airport, I finally found my bus and was soon happily in transit to my hotel. In Tokyo, the city of multiple personalities, I spent the next few days exploring this crowded but very organized city. Which each district makes you feel you are in an entirely different place. I was enjoying these days, especially with my rail pass - since it was much easier to explore by train. I always found traveling by train so interesting, so necessary for the aspect of learning the culture, society, and even to see the personalities of the place. This city was alive and full of action, and the people were to me the most respectful I have ever encountered in the world, which gave me a good feeling and some sense of belonging. I could easily get used to spending my time here in Tokyo.

One of the most amazing sights that I encountered in this city was that every late afternoon after the locals had finished work, you could notice as far as the eyes could travel a sea of black suits; it was a surreal sight. That was because here, all working men wore them for business, like a respect thing or to show that they were professional. I liked the sight and the professionalism of these locals, as it showed that they were somewhat devoted to their jobs and the rules of the workplace. I also imagined that they might be very hardworking men who followed every instruction given to them well by their superiors.

It was cold this time of the year in Japan, being the middle of the final stages of winter. My favorite thing to do at night, before I went back to my hotel, was to eat a bowl of hot ramen, which is a thick noodle soup. There were many sidewalk stalls to choose from. The hot ramen complemented the cold weather perfectly, and the taste was something I savoured. I realized that ramen was pretty popular among the Japanese people. Here, for 500 Yen or about $7 Australian dollars, I could slurp on the delicious ramen noodles any time I wanted. Another thing I noticed was that the locals slurped their ramen loudly. In Tokyo, it shows that they are enjoying the food. So, the louder you slurp the better you are enjoying the food. So, I also slurped well at this ramen sidewalk stall on my last night in Tokyo, not knowing when I would return to this inviting and hospitable city.

I tried a few other restaurants in Tokyo to get familiar with the city's cuisine and tastes. I vividly remember ordering Sashimi at one restaurant, and it was a very new experience for me. As the food came out on a plate with the fish still alive, flapping its tail slowly in the final stages of its life, I was surprised and intrigued. It was a truly fascinating sight and it also guaranteed that the food was fresh, but I was not sure whether the fish was feeling any pain or not. I had tasted many foods and visited many restaurants in different parts of the world, but an alive fish on a plate was something new to me. Needless to say, I enjoyed this experience and the freshness of the fish.

Now, my three days in Tokyo have come to an end. It was the day of my departure. I now had to go for my train trip to Fukuoka. So, catching my first train to Tokyo Station,

I then boarded a train called the Shinkansen, which is a bullet train. This train was so comfortable and smooth, and the food aboard was also good. My overall experience on the Shinkansen was great, with all the conductors and waiters bowing every time they entered and left my carriage. This trip had twenty stops including Osaka, Kyoto, and Hiroshima, which gave a sense of connection as to how all the cities here fitted together as a country. Aboard the train, I decided to randomly give out small Koala Bears as a gift to many passengers. I had bought about fifty of these very cheap unique Australian icons from the Gold Coast back in Australia, which the Japanese passengers all happily accepted. I also felt happy seeing them appreciate my kind gesture.

After some time, the train pulled into Fukuoka which was the last stop on the Shinkansen line. I traveled nine-hundred kilometers in just six hours and definitely enjoyed this train trip. I would describe my journey from Tokyo in Honshu Island in the North to Fukuoka in Kyushu Island in the South as serene and fast. I got off at the last stop and the station's name was Hakata. At the station, I bought one of the famous Hakata Dolls and then changed trains to Saga, which was a separate train line. It was a bit late by the time I arrived in Saga, so I planned to just have a good rest. Then I would get up and go to Cherry's club the next night and face up to whatever drama was forthcoming.

I did not realize where this brave heart came from? However, I was capable of bearing the roughness of this world, as I already did! It is not something new to my soul. My soul gets used to these sorts of things. Cherry's wind held me automatically to an ocean of waste. I only sailed without a compass. I was sailing without stopping. I sailed my whole life, always experiencing, always looking for something precious other than my kindness. Kindness to humanity is something pure. You could get mistaken by other people; you could be used! Kindness is not always a weakness. They had mistaken my kindness for my weakness. The wind of Cherry was bringing me that idea to my mind. The idea of being stupid because you are kind. Never! A stupid person is not kind.

The next day, I woke up and was refreshed from a good sleep. I started feeling more relaxed after my simple Lawson Station breakfast of eggs and rice, with a cup of hot coffee. Then, my afternoon was spent relaxing in a Japanese bath and sauna house. Already knowing the way and direction from my last trip to Saga, that night I easily found the club where Cherry worked without any worries or delay. I arrived at the club at about 10pm and, as usual, heard all the loud greetings again of "Irassahaimase!". My eyes circled slowly around the club and searched around like a submarine telescope and, at this time, I observed there were about eight Japanese men of various ages taking their turns at singing karaoke. Apart from them, there were some sexy young Filipino and Japanese girls wearing very short dresses, clapping and encouraging them to sing more. The overall atmosphere was that of pure bliss and happiness. Even though all the girls were obviously fake or tone-deaf, it did not matter to the Japanese singers. All that mattered to them was that they all thought they were singing with a voice like Frank Sinatra.

I was seated courteously by one of the sexy girls and another poured me a glass of Hennessy XO Cognac, which was from the bottle that I paid for from my last trip. In a moment, I felt like the Prince from the East, who was pardoning him a cup! A cup which he would never forget. The cup made him fall asleep in the rim of his life. He did not want to wake up, as everything was passing by, he just kept enjoying the cup, forgetting himself, forgetting that he was the son of the king.

Everything in this place was giving me a sign. A sign that Melodrama would happen, all my emotions were making me carry on and on until this all plays out. This is how my life was and it will be always. I love the pure things. And to show the purest of a thing you should take off the masks from the faces. Then I am now more curious than being an innocent kind person. While I was thinking about these things, I immediately requested Cherry to sit with me, and I also insisted on speaking to the club's manager, which was a request. The head lady seemed strange, judging by the expression on her face, and her appearance with her face full of very thick makeup. I would say that this lady was in her 50's, but in her mind, she probably believed that she was still in her late 20's, considering the way she was dressed.

Then by gazing at this lady, my mind was busy, I started to understand how people fall into their illusion. They live in the abyss of their world, but they feel the magnificence of this illusion flowing in their veins which keeps them very strange! They were just literally as a Japanese doll playing different roles, controlled by one. It is a shame when you believe the debased life that you have in your perfect life. I did not carry any feelings. However, these ideas were flashing in my mind very smoothly like a wild river that knows everything. I was calm and relaxed and did not know what to expect. And why should we expect such a thing while we are already on a journey? And how could I have known what was waiting for me?

Before long, a very tough man with two bodyguards was standing before me. He was a scary man with tattoos of dragons and snakes all over his arms, and there were tattoos even on his neck and bald head. This man was a member of the Yakuza, which is the equivalent to the Mafia in other parts of the world, or at least this is what they told me.

Maybe they were just trying to scare me; well, I can tell you that, if that was the case, they were doing a pretty good job.

Then, I started to explain to the tattooed boss man courteously that I wanted Cherry's passport and for her to come back to the Philippines with me. The manager's face changed, as though a typhoon had arrived on a sunny beach without warning. He got so angry and abusive, and even smashed his hand down on the table, spilling all the drinks. He then roared, "Get out of my club now and do not come back!" His tone and voice were very intimidating and, maybe it was the drink I had or just the feeling that I was being attacked for no reason, I also got angry and yelled back at him in response. Then, surprisingly, he seemed to calm down. Perhaps, he was surprised or shocked that I spoke back to him, as the feeling I got was that no one ever dared talk back to this boss man.

He walked away with his two poodles, as it seemed, but they were his bodyguards. Wherever this boss man went, they always followed. The voice inside my head urged me to leave everything and run because then I had a very bad feeling and did not know what to expect. Maybe they would kill me, but I think not inside this club that had a lot of witnesses. As long as there were people around, I felt that I was somewhat safe. After this encounter, the club went silent, and even loud breathing could be heard or, to coin a phrase, you could hear a pin drop. But I don't think that many people were carrying pins.

After what seemed like an eternity, the older lady came to the table, obviously instructed to do so by the angry stress happy manager. The good news was that she was an understanding person and seemed reasonable and had good people skills. By now, I think they all realized they would not be able to bully me. So, we talked for maybe two hours and she tried to persuade me to leave without

Cherry and even, at one stage, offered me a cash incentive and another girl for the night. She could not change my demands and I told her that I did not want trouble until, finally, they agreed that she could leave. But not for one month, until a replacement arrived. Although I had no trust, I had no choice as well, so I agreed. But I did insist that no drugs were to be given to Cherry over the next month. The lady also agreed that Cherry could have three days off and spend a little time with me before I left Japan. I allowed the manager to keep Cherry's passport with them, so they would believe we would not run away, and Cherry would be returned.

We shook on the deal. Cherry was sitting quietly, watching the whole scene with her dazed eyes. I did not understand her silence. I felt her shock and fear pushed her to this strange silence. That I felt somehow, she was satisfied with her current life. It is hard to convince someone who lives a shitty life - then in love with this shitty life - that there is a sweet calm life. I gazed for too long. Then I and Cherry departed the club back to my hotel room. In the room, we were both exhausted and I was worn out from stress.

We both slept virtually the instant we laid on the bed. And just like that, soon morning broke and a new day started. I was woken up by the beams of light peeking through the half-closed curtains. I squinted my eyes to adjust to the brightness. Today, I thought it would be a good idea to do a little sightseeing, and Cherry also agreed. So, seeing that I only had three days and with my sexy little devil, I hired a car and was also given some directions. The attendant at the car hire handed me the keys to a red Toyota Corolla. We were now in the hire car ready to leave. The attendant suddenly then walked to the middle of the road stopping all the traffic in both directions for us to have a clear path to proceed whilst bowing and waving goodbye, we were now on our way.

We were driving up to Nagasaki, a city where the Americans dropped the second atomic bomb in World War 2. It was quite a sad place and I noticed that the people of this town were rather unattractive and uglier than those in Saga, or any other place in Japan that I had visited. Maybe it was from the radiation fallout from the atomic bomb all those years ago.

We went to explore the Peace Museum which was full of all the facts of the fallout of the atomic bomb. It was amazing and very informative. The museum was built to educate people of the horrors of war and the threat of nuclear weapons, and mostly to teach the importance of peace. The mere thought of the ferocious heat and blast that indiscriminately slaughtered its inhabitants more than six decades ago made me shudder. It was scary to think that so many countries now have these devastating bombs built for the total destruction of the human race and could wipe out our world within days of a nuclear war. We tend to ignore these kinds of terrifying realities of life, but once you start thinking about it, it can be an extremely frightening and sobering reality. We spent hours at this peace museum, and it was well worth the visit.

The next day, I dropped my hired car back because I could not read the road signs in Japan. It was just a generally difficult job to drive in Japan because of the language barrier. We caught the train to a place called Huis Ten Bosch, which is a Dutch city like Amsterdam made into a theme park. I thought that it was unusual to have this theme park which seems to be in the middle of nowhere, but it was pretty popular - judging from the large number of visitors to this place. We spent a whole day at this theme park with all its splendors. It was a refreshing take from all the devastating yet interesting experiences we had the previous day. During the whole day, I kept feeling like I was in Holland with all its windmills. It was not until I left the exit, did I realize that I was not in Europe but Japan!

It was now late afternoon, so we caught the train up to Fukuoka and spent the night at a small hotel. It was located near the Hakata train station and was called the Green Hotel. The next day, Cherry would go back to Saga and me, well, I did not know as I had a month before Cherry would be able to return to the Philippines. I started to think about what my next destination would be for tomorrow. As this was our last night together, we wanted to enjoy as much as we could. So, we went partying at a local karaoke bar until the early hours of the morning. Feeling hungover and with a sore throat from singing out of tune the night before, I walked Cherry to the train station and bid her farewell until I would see her again, hopefully in a month or so. Well, as long as the club that she worked at and the boss man from the club also kept his word, I could see her.

Alone again, naturally, as the song goes, but I feel fine - which, strangely enough, sounds like another song. I was now feeling relaxed after the past week of stress. At this very moment, I was feeling so untroubled and serene, as if I did not have a care in the world. It was like a huge weight had been lifted off from my shoulders - the weight that was named Cherry. Still until today, I wonder why I pursued Cherry and complicated my life. There were so many things that I could have done differently, so many other women that I could have pursued, but I guess, it was out of my commitment that I stayed with Cherry. I was stupidly committed to this next chapter of my life.

I was starting to enjoy Japan with the friendly, warm, and calm people that inhabited this country. So, I decided that I would stay another night at Fukuoka in the Green Hotel alone. I spent my last day exploring the city and loved the friendly smiles from the local people. I had heard about the famous Fukuoka Castle as one of the must-see attractions in Japan, so I went on to find the castle to have a look. It was built in 1601 and even though I have seen many temples and castles before in many places, I was glad I decided to visit this attraction before leaving. So now, I was here at this awesome monument. Tranquility and serenity were what I felt at the remains of an ancient time in Japan. It made me see and feel the past at Fukuoka Castle. I reminisced about the Samurai times while exploring the remains. It is amazing how a simple yet meaningful artifact can evoke so many memories and hold so much importance. Soon, nightfall was upon me before I exited the relic to return to my hotel in the city.

I spent a quiet night at the Green Hotel alone where I relaxed with not a care in the world. I grew to love Japan and almost persuaded myself to stay here for the next month. Then again maybe staying would alert my presence to the Boss Man from Saga who I hoped never to focus my vision to his face ever again. Before my eyes closed into a "Rumpelstiltskin" type sleep or just a long sleep, my final decision before snoozing was Korea.

Chapter 14

KOREA.

I woke up with a tired body, but also with total excitement to explore. I was just finding my pleasure to know more people, to hear some other stories, touching the history of each place, living with the current life. I enjoyed the twists and turns with a big heart full of love. Although the harsh things will come, I already gave my heart to the wind. Therefore, whatever comes, let it come. I flew with the flow until I became the flow. Here I am, waking up with the sunbeams kissing my face, and the fresh morning air filling my lungs. I had decided to visit Korea and found my way to the pier. There, I caught the beetle boat which was a fast hydrofoil, or jet ferry as they called it here in Kyushu Japan. The boat trip between Fukuoka and Busan would take around three to four hours of travel time on the waters.

I was excited, my blood was running very fast carrying adrenaline that mixed my emotions with happiness, and thoughts of adventure that made me delighted. Since this would be my first ever trip to Korea, I was just happy as a child who will visit a new place - that keeps him awake all night. I already knew that Busan was a peaceful place that rises into a sea of mountains beyond as it was a port city with beaches, mountains, and temples. Needless to say, I was looking forward to staying in this country. On arrival, I made my way to the beautiful hotel named the Marriott Hotel, and I stayed at this hotel for three days. I made sure to enjoy the tranquility and peace of what this hotel had to offer. What's more, there were many beautiful and friendly girls who I had the pleasure to meet - that made my stay even more exciting and fun.

On my second day at the hotel, one of the girls at the reception invited me to visit Busan Tower with her. As a person who is very fond of sightseeing and this being my first time in Korea, I agreed to the girl's offer. She gave me a guided tour of the place and shared many details and information to go along with the visit. I enjoyed her company and the tour that she gave me, so I thanked her at the end of the day. Her kisses were quite inviting and all day she was holding my hand. I was not sure if she was being sweet or just making sure I never got lost. She was aware of my next destination, that was to Seoul, and asked to come with me as that was her place of birth. I did not know what to say to her request so I just remained silent and did not answer.

The next day, I spent my time relaxing and enjoying myself at the beach. There, I had the pleasure of meeting several Korean beauties and even flirted with some of them. It was an exciting day, and I also got to eat foods that were so fancy and delicious that they would easily be fit for the Emperor of the country. All in all, it was a day that couldn't get any better, and I was just generally enjoying being alive. I realized that my life, at that moment in time, was like a dream. A dream that I didn't want to end anytime soon. But sadly, all things do come to an end eventually.

After these enjoyable three days in Busan, it was time for me to leave and move on to my next stop, which was Seoul. It was a huge metropolis and the capital of South Korea. After a comfortable flight that went on for an hour towards the north, I then found myself in a new place. I had chosen to fly with Korean Airlines, which was a very welcoming airline and the plane was a comfortable 737. It did not take long to arrive, and all the way, I wondered why I went alone. Why had I resisted the advances of the hotel beauty, who wanted to accompany me on this trip? I guess this is how I wanted it. I was already committed to my young devil and of course, this was the reason. I had to be now faithful and strong but I knew all the time in my subconscious mind it would be the wrong decision.

After arriving in Seoul, I took a taxi ride to my hotel which was the JW Marriott. This was an amazing hotel and the comfort was as good as I could have stayed in. On my first day, I hung out at the hotel and checked out the city sights. I wanted to get familiar with this new place and see what it had to offer. The city was full of Buddhist temples and shopping malls, and there was also a huge casino in the city, full of big gambling locals. Seoul was giving the waves of culture with the food halls, and dance floors. Waving with history with widened gates and the future full of glass and steel towers. Seoul tells the story of tradition and contemporary life full of inspiration.

The highlight of my trip to Seoul was a trip to the North Korean border, just a one-hour van ride away from Seoul. The section in the middle was called "No man's land", a demilitarized zone. This, in itself, was amazing; however, the sad reality was that the people past this spot were North Koreans, who live a hard life similar to the Berlin wall. It was freedom on one side and oppression on the other. I felt somewhat sorry for the other side, but it was a trip that I did enjoy and thought it was something different, with propaganda blasting from loudspeakers. The reasoning for this, well, was something I could only guess. To be honest, and to put it quite bluntly, I felt that this was just another case of total human stupidity.

After the return trip from the border, I was once again in Seoul. There, I enjoyed the unique food, especially the Korean barbeque restaurants. The friendliness of the beautiful Korean girls, who were somewhat similar to Japanese but with straight legs. The girls were also a rather enjoyable memory of my visit to Seoul even though I never tasted any of these beauties. If you ask me why, I would not have the answer except for the fact I wanted to be faithful. I also sometimes wondered if Cherry was doing the same. In time I would realize that is one of the impossibilities of this world.

Another three days went by, and I decided to fly back to Manila before I ended up falling in love with a beauty from Korea - which, maybe, I should have but instead, I chose to returned to Manila where I would wait for the arrival of Cherry.

My flight to Manila was with Eva Air the Taiwanese Airline. My reasoning to fly with this airline was because it had a twenty-hour stopover in Taipei in transit to Manila. On arrival at Taiwan Taoyuan International Airport, I took the opportunity to visit the Beitou Hot Springs which was just a short train ride away from the city. Taiwan was under Japanese rule from 1895 until 1945 which is why this hot spring culture blossomed in this area. I relaxed and soothed my tired body in the Millenium Hot Springs and even though it was public bathhouse full of people from all walks of life, young and old, it was great and just another experience worth taking. At night I found a nice drinking pub and enjoyed talking to the locals who seemed a very intelligent race of people and all spoke good English unlike Japan. Next morning, I was back at the airport for my 7am flight to my next destination Manila Philippines.

Chapter 15

CAVITE MANILA.

On my flight I began to reminisce about Korea, it had given me such a relief to my soul that I needed, with all the beauty, the fresh cold air that brings so much of a feeling of peace and pleasure with all its friendly people it made me realize why Korea was called the "Land of the Morning Calm". I had now returned to Manila, where I had organized to meet Cherry's sister Edelyn once I arrived. I had met her before on the Super Ferry months earlier when I first met Cherry, but we were not well acquainted as yet. Well, that wouldn't be for long, as both of us soon started to find a place for us to stay together when Cherry arrives home.

We started searching for a place that would be suitable to live, in readiness for the arrival of Cherry. I settled for a place in a gated estate in Bacoor Cavite, not so far from SM City which are a hugely popular malls in the Philippines. There, we could also shop or just hang out whenever we wanted to. Even though Cavite was similar to a province, with the SM Mall nearby it would give the illusion we were actually in a city.

As I and Edelyn had become quite comfortable with each other at this point, Cherry's sister, of course, propositioned me for sex. I did not know from where did she come up with this idea that I wanted to have sex with her. I immediately refused, without thinking twice - not just because I was not attracted to her, but it would also have been a big insult to her sister and would have destroyed any future relationship with Cherry. I should have realized at that very moment that the sister of Cherry had bad morals and should not be trusted. We became good friends instead and worked together to get ready for Cherry's arrival. Out of nowhere, Edelyn convinced me to open up a bridal boutique for her, which was not so far from SM City, along Aguinaldo Highway.

I, once again being naïve and unaware of her clever tricks, stupidly trusted her and invested $5,000 American dollars to set the boutique up. The reasons I trusted her were like the words of a Rodriguez song "She had the answers that made my questions disappear". In hindsight, her words were just like a politician's promise. I later learned that Edelyn, the sister, already had three boutiques in Cagayan De Oro. When I agreed to her request to open up a bridal boutique, what I was thinking was that it would be ok since it would keep Cherry busy when I would be away sometimes in Australia.

It did not take long for another three weeks to pass, and sure enough, my sweet Cherry now had arrived in Manila. I met her at the Philippine Airlines Terminal 2. I gave her a warm kiss with a tight hug. I was so surprised that she also had three large suitcases with her and I had no idea what was inside them all. I said nothing and then proudly took her up to the new house that I had arranged for us to stay in. She seemed happy with the house that Edelyn and I had found. Upon learning about the new bridal boutique, Cherry was even more surprised and delighted. The boutique was named "Edelyn's", and even though I could have thought of a better name, I just went along with her wishes - that was to be expected since I was submissive.

A few days had passed since the arrival of my girl Cherry from Japan, and our days had been going great in the beginning, but I soon started noticing that she would always get sick in the morning. The morning sickness was getting quite frequent. So, I decided to take her to the doctor nearby our house. After examination and some tests, the doctor confirmed my worst nightmare, that Cherry was pregnant. Not only that, she was due next June! Cherry then assured me that I was the father and, of course, I believed her. After all, she did say I was the only man she has had sex with for over two years which I naively thought she was telling the truth.

Cherry and I spent the next two months living in our little house in Cavite. During this time, we were just living a simple life, without any major parties or trips. Sometimes though, we would visit karaoke bars and have a little fun. After all, Cherry was a good singer and enjoyed these places a lot. I guess this is what she did in Japan where she worked, as she did feel good and happy singing and getting claps and cheers from the crowd. I was not a singer; I just drank and felt stupidly proud sitting with her, enjoying her company.

I was not giving so much attention or noticing myself sinking into her deceptive happy-go-lucky lifestyle. With my blurry eyes, I did not notice how she climbed to me very easy, and how things are getting very fast. Things happen! Yes. However, it is not like this speed. The Godspeed that makes you always running with a specific rhythm without knowing why? without knowing what you are doing, you are just running. I found myself running with this little naughty liar girl with a slow-motion life. This contradiction created a very weird circumstance in my current life.

Chapter 16

LUZON TRAVEL AND BRIDAL BOUTIQUE.

Time was passing slowly in Cavite, and to break the same events that were racing our life with strange haste I needed a change, now the travel bug was biting my feet hard. So, Cherry and I decided to go on a trip up to Angeles City. There, I could also go to visit my old friend, Vic Diaz. When the trip was organized, we planned to stay in the Swagman Hotel in Balibago, just out of the middle of the City, and the notorious Fields Avenue where all that part of town was full of bars where you could find any naughty thing that you desired.

Angeles City had the name which the locals affectionately called it "The City of Angels". This city was evacuated in 1991 and almost destroyed by the fallout from the Mount Pinatubo volcano eruption which was the largest volcanic eruption of the 20th century. The Swagman was like a little resort for Australians, and the best and safest way to get there was to catch a bus called Fly the Bus. This bus departed three times a day, from the sister Swagman Hotel located at Ermita Manila. The bus trip took two hours and they always played a movie on the bus TV, along with serving other things - such as beer, soft drinks, and snacks if needed for the trip.

Before long, we boarded this big blue bus to finally start our journey. Cherry and I noticed that the large bench seat at the back of the bus was not taken. So, we chose to sit there together. Soon, Cherry and I started drinking some beers and started getting relaxed as time passed by. Before the movie started, there was a little Tagalog lesson on the bus TV screen and it said, in Tagalog, that "Love equals Mahal and Mahal equals Expensive too", so that meant that love is expensive. In my opinion, not a truer statement on life could be said.

I noticed that the bus became a little dark as the curtains were drawn because of the movie. Now, the volume coming from the movie had been turned up louder too and you could hardly see or hear what was happening around inside the bus. So, my Cherry, being the naughty girl that she was, decided to take advantage of the moment. Without asking, she started giving me the Linda Lovelace impersonation. At first, I was startled and tried to stop her, but then I just succumbed to her deep throat sucking on the back seat. This girl was very good at what she did, and well, I couldn't complain. Then, I also started rubbing her very slowly, trying to touch her very softly between her warm thighs, and before long, had her pushed against the bus window very gently in an excited manner.

Now, I was pushing inside this naughty girl as hard as possible, but without too much noise, just with a nice moaning sound and that made me push deeper and faster, as we were totally now out of the context of the bus. We acted as if it were just us together on the bus and no other passengers. I suddenly jumped with shock when a soft voice said "Would like another beer Sir?" It was the bus waitress, to my surprise. I was amazed and shocked that she had the courage or confidence to interrupt our sex, but I said "Okay!" and ordered two San Miguel beers. The young hostess did not seem to care about what we were doing. Maybe she had seen it all before and had now become accustomed to these types of events on board. Still, it was a pretty interesting encounter. When the waitress returned with the beer, I handed Cherry her beer as we continued what we were doing. Now, we were also drinking our beer at the same time, as if we were in a private place like our own lounge room. This went on for a while until I was ready to climax, we were also nearing our destination, so I turned her around and filled her mouth, so much that it spilled out from the sides of her mouth. She then simply washed it down with the rest of her beer and smiled.

We had arrived at our destination now and, needless to say, the bus trip was an experience that would always be remembered as not your ordinary bus ride. Getting off the bus, I collected our bags and then checked in to this simple hotel. The good times were now beginning, and I was way too excited for what was to come. In a happy mood, I went inside the big restaurant area of the complex and, there, sitting and smiling was my dear old friend, Vic. I greeted him in a very pleasant manner and introduced him to Cherry. I was feeling really good once again, as Vic had always been good company. We sat all night talking about life and updates that occurred in the last days, we enjoyed every second with smiles and laughter, as we also ate delicious food that gave to the joyful moments of the night, while we were listening to the hotel band playing in the background.

It was an amazing night with my old mate Vic. We had a beautiful friendship, very simple, very unique, we were telling each other only jokes and crazy things. Our friendship remained very cool. The next night, I left Cherry at the hotel while Vic and I, also a couple of other fellows from the hotel went up to explore Fields Avenue. In a nutshell, the place was alive and buzzing! With bars and bars full of beautiful young Philippine girls dancing on the stage and sliding up and down doing pole dancing, and tempting any full-blooded man to fall in love with them, even if it was just for the night. These girls were young and beautiful, and looked like they could tell more lies and had more tricks than I had ever dreamed of in my wildest dreams. Their main objective was to milk customers for as much as they could, to earn some cash for their own desires, or to send to their parents, grandparents, or even their boyfriends. What they needed the money for was something I could only wonder, but one thing I knew was that these girls were willing to do anything to get that money.

We had a few great days in Angeles, and before I knew it, it was now time to leave and catch another bus to our next destination. Now, we were headed toward Subic Bay, which was another bus ride from the Swagman Balibago. It was a place where, years earlier, the US Navy had a large contingent of soldiers here. The trip was short and took only two hours. Even though the numbers of US soldiers were maybe ten percent of what it was, it still attracted a lot of girls to come here in hopes of finding a husband or a boyfriend, or even someone generous or stupid enough to support her schooling or her family. In most cases, this was a very big commitment as some girls had as many as ten brothers and sisters, parents, and grandparents and some of the siblings already had children who needed food, schooling, and clothing.

After a few days here at Subic, I learned with a little disappointment that it was just a beach that had dirty water and garbage on the shore washed in from the ocean. People say that it is a beautiful beach, but although I did try to swim on the beach once, the smell of sewerage forced me back to the shore. It was nowhere near enjoyable, let alone beautiful, as I had heard. The dirtiness and smell of this place were enough to drive me out of there.

Then, we traveled up to La Union the Surf Capital of Luzon, where we stayed at a little surf camp just west of San Fernando. This location was quiet or "Tahimik" in Tagalog and I spent my time here surfing and becoming tanned in the warm sun. Once again, I had the pleasure of coming across many friendly locals. It was a pleasing change to get away from the hustle and bustle of crowds.

After a few days, we were off again and our next stop was Baguio the Summer Capital of the Philippines, which took another hour of journey. The trip was taken up the mountain from La Union. The city of Baguio was always cold, with a harrowing trip for one hour driving up a steep and mountainous narrow highway, giving the driver no room for error - as an accident here was not even an option. The drop was straight down with no chance of survival if we left the road. I nervously rode every corner on the mountain climb, and sometimes closed my eyes when an overtaking car or bus just had time to get back on the right side of the road before hitting head-on with an oncoming vehicle.

The Swagman had another hotel in Baguio and after a nerve-wracking bus ride, we arrived safely. It seemed that all the praying by the passengers had worked. This hotel was warm and inviting, and we spent our nights sitting by the open fire, drinking and listening to the band playing love songs. Also, in the daytime, we went to Burnham Park. There, we hired a rowboat and went boating around the lake in the center of the park. Then, we hired a couple of bikes and rode them around the park until dusk. Generally, we just enjoyed feeling young in this mountain city and it was a good break, away from the hot climate below. I had a lot of fun boating and riding bikes along the park that I didn't realize how much time we had been away from Cavite.

Time had been passing by so quickly with our travels, and I suddenly realized that we were away for three weeks from our house in Cavite. I didn't even notice that it had been so long, so I thought it would be better to go back now. Daylight came and we left from the local bus station with an eight-hour bus trip ahead of us before arriving home. I was not looking forward to the trip down the mountain, so onboard I closed the blinds and my eyes, and imagined that we were not descending the perilous mountain. It was a tiring and long bus trip; I was exhausted by the end of it and planned to spend the next day just relaxing in the house. However, other things were waiting for me.

I arrived very tired, but once I turned my keys to open the door, I was surprised to find three young girls who were in our house. I was confused why they were there because I didn't recall inviting anyone nor did I recognize these girls' faces. Well, they said that Cherry's sister, Edelyn, had invited them over to stay for a while. That wasn't a problem for me, but it would have been nice if she had asked me first for approval to stay. Well, I guess, this just showed her disrespect towards me or the confidence that she could do whatever she wanted. My biggest example was yet to come.

The next day, I was astounded with even more surprises, as when we went to the bridal boutique, all the shelves and hanging spaces were empty, more than two-hundred gowns were not there! I was shocked that Edelyn could be too careless with the boutique. I approached her and upon asking what was happening, Edelyn said that she sent them to Cagayan De Oro. There, they would be washed and cleaned. It seemed very strange to me, considering that city was over a thousand kilometers away. However, Edelyn insisted that they were the only ones who knew how to clean the dresses. I looked at her and actually half-believed her, knowing full well that it was a lie. The reason she was lying, I wasn't able to comprehend.

Yesterday was full of puzzles that made me confused and felt something was going on without having any idea! So today I went back to the boutique to see how the situation had played out or if the gowns were returned yet, cleaned and washed. However, what I saw left me in even more shock and surprise. It would be safe to say that I wasn't expecting this at all! Inside the boutique, there were now new owners inside, who were stocking the boutique with gowns. As for Edelyn, she had completely vanished, as if she had disappeared into thin air overnight. I realized that she had secretly sold my business behind my back, and I felt total betrayal. All the money and effort spent on this boutique that I opened for her, she just tossed it aside like it was nothing! I considered that amazing and so evil. How could she lie to me like that, sell something I had so readily made for her, and deceive me so easily? I was so angry, but what could I have done? What could I do at that very moment? The answer was nothing, but I realized how my trust and helpful nature was just being abused by this evil lady.

In a week, I had to go back to Australia to take care of my own business back there. So, I had to make decisions for our future, Cherry's and mine, before leaving. We decided to move out of the Cavite house and I sent Cherry to Cebu, where we had decided now to live. Cebu is the capital of the Visayas and was a nice city. It was nowhere near as crowded as Manila. Cherry would find a place there to rent and also furnish it, while I went home to Australia.

My divorce from Pamela in Australia was now complete, we had to separate for one year before this became final. In my mind, also as crazy as it seemed, I was planning to marry Cherry before the baby was born. I wanted the baby to have my name and also to commit myself completely to Cherry and our life together. So, being slightly wiser now,

I also prepared a prenuptial agreement in Australia. I had to have it signed by Cherry on arrival back in Cebu, before our wedding day.

Chapter 17

MARRIAGE AND BIRTH OF MY SON.

I spent the next two months in Australia doing my business and organizing all that was necessary to set up my business so I could stay away for long periods of time. After some months and a lot of effort, I had now finally arrived back in the Philippines. This time, I landed in Cebu where my new life would begin. It was a tough two months in Australia, but I was able to tie up all my unfinished business, and now had a clear mind, or at least this is what I thought in my mind for now. I was not sure if my plans for marriage were a good idea but it was my decision and the right thing to do. Maybe something big was waiting for me with the naughty Cherry but after all, she was pregnant and I wanted my son to have a father with him and I needed to give my son my name. Although my mind was in complete peace, a feeling always visited me to have a suspension about my future life. A life that I wanted to have with all the calmness, with all the simplicity. This feeling was making me feel uncomfortable from time to time but my decision was made so I just moved forward with a positive thought.

Cherry, who was now about seven months pregnant, also had found a nice little townhouse to rent near the beach at a place called Liloan. This place was about an hour away from Cebu City, if the journey was done by jeepney. Upon arrival, I noticed that this place was peaceful and tranquil, with no drama or troubles happening around. The house was also cozy and comfortable. We would live there together and make it our family home. Cherry and I enjoyed the peace here, where at night we would sit in a gazebo down by the beach and drink some beers with my Japanese neighbor, with whom we became good friends.

I was in shock when sadly, our neighbor had a heart attack one night. We had become too close at this point and the news of his sudden death, at the age of only forty, was a huge shock for me. It was very sad, especially when I realized that he had left his young wife and children alone now, I felt even sadder that my heart was sinking into deep sorrows for this man's young children and his widow. They would now have to face life's challenges alone. From time to time, I did miss drinking with this Japanese neighbor but soon came to terms with his death. Well, that is how life works; you never know when your time will come, or your neighbor's. I just hoped that his family found a way to cope with it.

As for Cherry's and my life, about three times a week, we would travel by jeepney to the Marriott Hotel in the city. The hotel was near Ayala, a beautifully designed shopping center - or mall as they called it there - with many outdoor restaurants. It also had picturesque landscaping, and even a waterfall in the middle of the four-story building. I had a gym membership at the Marriott, so I would swim and work out from time to time, to keep my mind and body refreshed and active. After lunch, we would also go to Holiday Massage nearby and I would have a shiatsu massage from a well-trained masseuse, which was just the greatest thing for a tired body. I met a lot of American ex-pats at the Marriott gym and their stories were amazing, even though I guess some were a little hard to believe. Nevertheless, I enjoyed listening to these stories and their experiences, regardless of if they were true or made up.

On the way home, which we would mostly travel by taxi, I noticed a place on one of my trips back home to Liloan. There was a club called the Koala Club and I became curious and interested to visit this new place I had found. Most days, I started stopping by and having a beer with the owner of the club from Sydney, named Ian. We had become good friends quickly as we were both from Australia and I liked having conversations with him and a beer from time to time. Ian was a retired train driver and a nice bloke to chat with about Australia, and we reminisced about many Australian customs together. Yes, I had to say that life was good at this point, and I was enjoying my newfound peaceful lifestyle.

Time was moving slowly but surely, and it was now two weeks before the expectancy of our baby. We had made arrangements at Liloan City Hall to get married and to give my son my name. I had finally decided to go with my stupid decision of marrying Cherry, which seemed not so stupid at the time, and she agreed in a response. Since I was married before in Australia, we had to have a civil marriage. I did meet with the Cebu Monsignor first to try to get married in the Catholic Church but seeing the huge amount of money that this corrupt man wanted and demanded, I refused and turned down his offer. Of course, that made everyone think that I was some kind of bad guy or disrespectful, but I have to tell you, this Monsignor Paul as he called himself was an extremely greedy and evil man. It was even well known in Cebu that this man had sex with underage girls and also sometimes boys. Yet, they all turned a blind eye to this and he was allowed to continue his exposure and even had fathered three children to sixteen-year-old girls. Amazing, and yet, they all thought I was the bad man and he was a saint.

We were able to have a nice little ceremony with the mother of Cherry and two of her friends as witnesses. All went well, even though the Judge arrived three hours late and was smelling of alcohol through and through. Following the shotgun wedding at the Liloan Town Hall, where we were married off by a drunken Judge, Cherry and I had planned to stay at the Marriott Hotel for two weeks as it was close to the hospital. Also, I was not comfortable at our current location as it was too far out of town. Finally, in June, 2001, my son was born. He was a beautiful baby and a very good boy. We called him Geoffrey after his dad, with the middle name being the maiden name of Cherry. It was the tradition here in the Philippines that the child's middle name would be the mother's family name. So, that was it, and really in truth, I did not have a problem with it. The main thing was that I now had a junior and it was a happy time and a good feeling.

We went back home to Liloan after only two days in the hospital. It was obvious now, and not practical for us to live far from town. So, one month after my son's birth, we both decided to move closer to Cebu City. We searched and looked around, and before long, we found another townhouse in Banilad. This one was on a quiet street at the back of Country Mall. We also hired a "Yaya" or helper, and babysitter for Cherry as this is what people do in this country. Unlike in Australia, where the mothers did all the housework and took care of the baby without any help, most mothers hired helpers here. At least, it gave me and Cherry a little freedom to go out sometimes for dinner and movies, or even a drink at a nice bar outside of the mall called Drifters. It was mostly frequented by ex-pats of many countries and was a happy and friendly place to spent a night with other foreigners.

As time passed, and so did my life with Cherry in Banilad, I started to have what I thought were heart attacks. I would frequently and regularly experience a shortness of breath and chest tightness. The first time when this happened, it was an experience that was scary and at one point, I was convinced that I was on my last breaths of life. I remember rushing to Chong Hua Hospital in a taxi, which was thirty-minutes away from our townhouse, and I was extremely nervous. This nervousness added to my already terrible health condition and I started having difficulty of breathing. On arrival, I was rushed straight into emergency and many wires were placed on my chest. I had no idea what was happening, as I was only forty-one and was physically fit. This happened on at least three occasions, but all seemed okay and they said that they were not heart attacks. I was to find out, years later, that Cherry was poisoning me but the Yaya at the time said nothing. I guess that was because she was scared or had been sworn to secrecy.

After three months in this Banilad townhouse, I was looking around to buy a place and was taken by a local agent to City Lights. There were two towers of condominiums on the way to Tops, which was the highest part of Cebu City in Nivel Hills. I wanted a unit with three bedrooms but they had only two-bedroom units for sale. I was about to leave and then the agent advised me that there was a penthouse in Tower 2 for sale. I immediately thought that this was out of my price range but still decided to view the unit. The penthouse was a beautiful two-story unit on the top two floors of Tower 2 with sweeping majestic panoramic views right across Cebu City, with the ocean in the distance. The agent was asking for 15-Million Pesos for the penthouse and, for some reason, I said "I will give you half" - thinking that maybe she would meet me halfway or at least give a discount.

Surprisingly, I was able to buy the beautiful penthouse for 8-Million Pesos, which was close to half of the original cost. I think they were desperate to sell this as this was the time of the Asian Crash of 2001. I also bought a new white Honda CRV car for our travels and journeys. Our life was getting better and Cherry seemed happier than ever. There were no trips to the Chong Hua Hospital anymore which was also very pleasing for me. Maybe, for now, Cherry did not want me dead or, at least, not yet. I was very stupid to fall for this devil woman and playing into her evil plans. Sometimes, I even hallucinated that I saw little horns protruding from this devil's forehead, just above her bulging Satan lookalike eyes.

Before long, I was living in a magnificent penthouse with Cherry and my newborn son. Soon, the maids went from one to three as it seemed that Cherry had now become a very Madam styled woman. She needed many servants, and she was also starting to change her attitude. I had my suspicions that she was cheating on me but it would not be until years later that I learned about the actual amount of sex this girl was having behind my back. I remember on one occasion, I had curtains installed in our home and remember coming home unannounced. Then, as I entered the house, I heard a lot of shuffling upstairs and noticed that our bed which was once made, was a little messy. I suspected many tradespeople working in the penthouse, such as mirror installers and tilers, who were all giving a little extra service to my wife. Still, I said nothing but realized I was turning a blind eye to the obvious.

We also needed to have our penthouse blessed and I was surprised, after my gym workout, to find that the priest had arrived early on a Saturday. Surely, he was not also having some extra delights with my wife. Before long, about twenty more people arrived and the party began.

The house blessing was a party day which all in attendance were seemingly happy, especially with the food and drinks. During the house blessing, I patiently listened to some insincere speeches from many of the guests. At the end of the party, I was relieved it was over.

Chapter 18

BAPTISM PARTY IN ALONA BEACH BOHOL.

In the middle of all these events, I did not notice how things had been changing rapidly. Even right before my eyes, Geoff was approaching one year of age. It is crazy how quickly time passed! You just are in the middle of the race - then all of sudden the race was over and you figured out that you were at full speed, sometimes racing with yourself, sometimes with love, and sometimes with hate. The sweetness of these events that I am living would give me a quiet life. Or just would keep blinding my eyes, and keep riding the ride. Cherry insisted that we go on a trip to Bohol for a baptism party for my son, Geoff. After all, my little man was growing up pretty fast. And of course, to keep Cherry happy, I agreed to her demand. She also explained that this was the tradition in the Philippines but in my mind, there was more to this trip than the tradition.

The baptism would have to be in Bohol, as many of Cherry's family members lived there. So, after it was all planned and settled, we travelled from Cebu to Bohol by Ocean Jet with my friend Nick from Australia and my other American friend Nick from Texas; Both of them were in agreement to be Godfathers of my son. I thought it was a good idea considering the hospital trips I endured months earlier. I still hoped that whatever was the reason, my body was now over it.

We had booked Nipa Huts, which were a small traditional Philippine house with straw roofing and bamboo walls, and a unique verandah. It was booked at Alona Beach, which was a little resort that was about forty-minutes by taxi from the Tagbilaran City boat terminal. We filled four taxis as there were many well-wishers at the pier to greet us. Maybe the word was out that Santa Claus was coming back to town. After arriving at the resort, we unpacked our bags and had a little swim in the ocean before meeting up with my two friends named Nick the Godfathers at the hotel bar later in the afternoon.

We started having some drinks and the whole first night was spent drinking with my friends and the locals. The locals were very amicable, especially when I said my wife was a Filipina; or maybe they were just full of crap, so they could get a few free drinks. This place was full of foreigners from America and Europe, and they all liked to drink and chase girls. It was apparent that they loved to tell their stories about how good of lovers they were and about their many conquests. I said nothing and just listened to these old men fooling themselves, but it was okay. At least they seemed happy and most probably were learning what I would learn in my future with Cherry. I now wonder who tricked them also.

The next day, we travelled only minutes for the baptism ceremony at the local church. It was a historical relic from the Spanish days. It was a really beautiful church, full of history and gave a very spiritual feel inside, with its sandstone block walls and timber ceilings and decorations down to a realistic statue of the crucifix of Jesus Christ.

The ceremony was a simple one, the priest splashed water on my son's head, and with a short prayer and a payment of 2,000 Pesos to the priest, he said "You are now living in the house of God". Following the baptism, we all went back to our resort where we were staying. Cherry had arranged a baptism party at the restaurant of Alona Beach Resort where we were staying. The food was plentiful with two whole Lechons and many cartons of San Miguel beer. I could not help but wonder why there were so much food and beer, and suddenly, I was no longer wondering as a jeepney arrived full of Filipinos with at least forty people loaded onboard. Some were even on the roof of the arriving jeepney. I was also amazed how the jeepney's tyres did not puncture as they were all virtually flat because of the weight of the passengers.

These people were ready to drink and eat with smiles from ear to ear. I actually thought that I heard some of the visitors call me Santa but surely, I was just hearing things. I also noticed that the priest from the baptism was also there and led the prayers which lasted about twenty-minutes and with another 2,000 Pesos in his hands, it seemed that God had blessed the party. It was a great party, which was more like a fiesta with singing and dancing until the early hours of the morning.

When the party-goers all finally left, not one person said thank you but passed just a few murmurs of "God is Good". I could not help but notice that the priest also had a room at the resort and was being accompanied to his room by two pretty girls - maybe they were planning late-night bible studies. The next day, it was time to return to Cebu but Cherry, to my surprise, again had planned a trip on the way home. This time to Loboc River, where a boat was awaiting us all to arrive. There was another buffet lunch and a band on board. And guess what, another surprise! A jeepney full of people arrived again, most of them were from the baptism party the night before.

I did not realize that Cherry had so many friends and relations. Another fiesta of food, drinks, and singing with the band followed. As nightfall fell upon us, we needed to head back to the Ocean Jetboat terminal for our trip back to Cebu, where we arrived within minutes to spare for the departure.

I believe that I am a fair person, but this baptism weekend cost me about $5,000 Australian dollars. I could not help but think that these people took advantage of the kindness of what they thought was Santa Claus. I never complained or said a word, although I did feel so stupid and used. I swore no way would I ever return to that place again.

Chapter 19

BRIDAL BOUTIQUES AND FASHION DESIGN COURSE.

It was not too long after arriving back from the baptism and renovating our new home with beautiful and colourful decors and new wall painting, everything was almost new. Also now, for our next project to embark on, a bridal boutique, and before long there was the opening of the bridal boutique for Cherry which we would call "Cherry's Bridal Fashions". I do not know where this brand name came from. However, it seemed obvious, and I think! it is suitable for the whole concept of the boutique. I found a perfect location about a five-minute walk from Ayala Mall for our first boutique. The boutique was a twenty-minute drive from our Penthouse at City Lights. It was on the T-Junction of Gorordo Avenue and Ayala Road, where you can hear all the noisy traffic and sound of the motorcycles filling up the atmosphere and all the people heading up towards their own business, dancing in harmony inside your ear.

The building was a rundown little old shop, so with the help of others, I professionally altered the roof and I tiled the floor perfectly with a nice pattern. As well as for windows putting them at the front with cover for security at night, and the final touch was some nice couthy change rooms and lighted signs at the front. The business was utterly ready to go. Without any doubt, it required a priest's blessing and a party to finalize the grand opening of the boutique. The priest was called to do the job, as the food was ordered and of course, once again people arrived to eat. I was not sure if it was my imagination, but I noticed the priest and other guests seemed to be gaining weight.

With all this now done, Cherry had her boutique and she seemed happy at least for today. The gowns they made here were extremely fashionable and magnificent with high quality fabrics. She employed about eight people which two of them were doing the beadwork designs on the gowns. These bead workers were too patient as their hands were so artistic to embroider a tiny detail with suitable colours, they were spending up to almost one week to make the pattern of the gown perfect. All seemed to be going smoothly, and I was enjoying the freedom. I spent more time playing golf, and generally just hanging out most nights. My routine was to pick up Cherry, then we would eat dinner at Ayala Mall. She was seemingly happy with this arrangement.

As time passed, It was not long before we had three boutiques, good workers, and business was becoming profitable. Although any money made was quickly spent by the waster Cherry. I was a little confused that she then wanted to do a fashion design course in Manila to become a designer which was a two-year course at a college in Makati. I do not know where this idea came from, but I tried to tell her to wait a year, however she persuaded me to agree. Well! I had no choice, as I basically said no but the drama became too much from this woman, hence I said yes. I then flew to Manila and bought her a small studio condominium in a tower called Makati Palace which was in the corner of Burgos Street Makati which was near to the red-light district. The studio unit was small but was also well designed and I tried to arrange almost everything with new painting and new aesthetic decors. I renovated it and decorated it perfectly with the help of my cousin Dave, who came from Australia to help me out.

The deal was Cherry would stay in Makati with the Yaya and fly home every second week to Cebu. She would arrive on a Friday night and leave on a Monday morning. Therefore, this was now how we lived. Everything had been debased. I never saw her much. When she was in Cebu, usually on Fridays and Saturday nights, she was out spending almost all the night at the disco until 2am. She thought only of herself, she is self-indulgent, frivolous and lacking in devotion. Cherry was acutely letting down people, which is driving her to scheme and manipulation. She now had no interest in me at all, she merely considered me as her supply of money. It did not take too much time for our marriage to become a joke. She appeared to have no sincere feelings at all about the marriage itself or our son Geoff.

She came across as straightforwardly cold and brutish, and Cherry treated me like trash with no respect in the slightest. She had now become so full of herself and thought she was Miss World. But actually, she was just now a "Bigaon" or in English a cheating slut always. The two helpers that Cherry hired now became far too disrespectful and lazy. They slept half the day, therefore I had to make them leave. So, I hired two new ladies. They helped me take care of Geoff my son, cooked and cleaned the Penthouse. My time was spent playing golf and generally just enjoying the dream life as a free man.

I was living a dream life with no wife around to annoy me. I just played golf with my Korean and Japanese lady friends. They were so good to me, as we had happy days playing at the Mactan Airforce golf course a thirty-minute drive from my condo in Nivel Hills. The golf course was also very close to Mactan Airport. There was no sex involved, just friendship and these ladies could play well a lot better than me. But my game did improve over time.

Whilst in Cebu I started to set up a business in Singapore with Gary, as the Australian business was going ok as I had two good employees answering the phone, printing, and banking the cheques in Australia. After three months of planning and setting up websites in 2003, I met Gary in Singapore. We began business and my stupidity would bite me seven-years later, as Gary ran the bank account and he helped himself to thousands and thousands of dollars. So now Singapore's direct mail business was underway. I would print and courier two thousand letters per week by FedEx and my employee in Singapore would mail the letters.

In later years, I found out the FedEx boy that collected the boxes was having sex with Cherry. Actually! maybe all the boys in Cebu were having sex with Cherry without my knowledge. Even people texted me anonymously and some even told me to my face not to trust her, it just seemed I did not care, maybe kidded myself it was not true.

Chapter 20

CHERRY AND HER BOYFRIEND.

After all these things happened, I then got a call from Carlos the son of Vic my old friend telling me was in a bad way. He had a stroke. All he could do is stay in his house totally confined to bed, he was now not well. I wanted to go visit my dear old friend in Manila so I got organized and went to the airport for a noon flight. After arriving at Manila Airport, I promptly hired an airport taxi to visit my good friend. It was too sad to see this cheerful man this way, struggling in his agony. He had lost a lot of weight; you could see this obviously by his sunken face and he had become very pale. He passed all his time sitting in bed with the help of his nurse. I've been expecting to spend a lot time with my friend Vic, enjoying our time as we did have planned, but life always brings us winter instead of spring, you just keep standing in front of this whole thing without doing anything.

I felt incapable and somehow seeing my friend in this situation made me feel like my soul had sunk into despair. I spent a few hours with Vic, also I spoke to his wife. And when I left, my heart started being in such sorrow. I already knew this would be the last time I would see my friend alive. One of the emotions that still has an impact on me is to lose a friend, a friend with his smile, his crazy things, his ambition to entertain people, his face when he sees you, his little secrets that he used to tell me. I do not know if these things will vanish with time but my friend Vic would be always on my mind. I bid my farewell.

I carried my body leaving Vic with all emotions and memories that we had together, I was still thinking about him. Subsequently, I preceded to my condo where Cherry was staying at Makati Palace for an unannounced visit. I found there were so many men's clothes in the wardrobe. I then went downstairs and had a talk with the head guard and asked him "Do you ever see my wife with other boys?" he replied shamefully not being able to look me in the eyes "Sir better you find another wife". I then waited for Cherry until she arrived at the Makati Condo. I opened the window which allowed the northerly breeze to enter the unit. The condo was a cozy place with good light and a good view across the skyline. I started pacing back and forth waiting for Cherry to arrive with composure and irritation. Once she arrived as she opened the door, she saw me wholly in front of her at the door, she was truly shocked like she saw Azrael.

I immediately confronted her with a question "Who owns these men's clothes?". She said ludicrously "They are my brother Elson's clothes". She was such a good liar and I started seeing all her lies in her eyes. I got to know how to subdue this evil. I added saying "But Elson lives in Cebu?". All of sudden, she said warily waiting for me to believe her. "Yes! but he was coming to Manila soon, therefore he sent his clothes ahead." My reply was "Ah Ok!" maybe to show her this stupidity of mine although I knew everything, I knew her drama, her lies, her small tiny detail of her face when she wanted to conceal something. However, to show my stupidity or to let her think this way as almost everything about such a story makes you know it is all made up. She must have been surprised how stupid I was to believe her. Really her story and reasons about the men's clothes did not add up.

I then asked Cherry, "Where is the Yaya that was staying with you here in the condo supposedly taking care of you?" - after all that was what I paid her for. She swiftly replied "Ruby was a slut. She was never here all the time. She would always be out staying in different places and in the end, I had no other option but to throw her out. She had so many boys and now is pregnant." It was far too obvious with this lie that this Devil Girl Cherry was just a habitual liar with a hard-hearted persona lurking and eluded, as she did not notice that she was more accessible because of her lies, then she thought that she deserves compassion unto the slightest. However, she merely ended up building a very tangled web of lies. I remained quiet beneath her lies. I did not want to manifest that I already knew what is under her mask, I'm just waiting for the right moment to expose the charade of this devil woman. So, I had arranged the next day to meet Ruby in secrecy to reveal this drama play which is directed by Cherry.

Ruby texted me to meet each other. She wanted to go home to Bohol because Cherry was living with a boy named Darwin, thus she could not stay with her. The name Darwin was in my mind as I wanted to pull more details from Ruby. So, I pretended that I'm surprised about this name. I only repeated the name after her: "Darwin?" - with a voice full of curiosity and sincerity. She started talking about this boy Darwin. He worked at the Renaissance Hotel in Greenbelt, which was a part of Makati City. Moreover, she said they were always having shabu which is a crystal drug, and then partying. Also, Darwin was only one of many boys that Cherry had sex with. I continue hearing the same old stories over and over again, with her bitterness in my throat I kept hearing all the words of Ruby whilst being calm to do not stand up and headed up toward the Renaissance Hotel and kill this pawn.

I started at the same time to become bitter towards Cherry, she was not a sweet Cherry. I could have done so many things only for her. I've been a blind-heart without any doubt that makes me not see who really, she is. She is a serpent in the form of a human being, although she poisons me, I'm still here alive, living all the lies, all the suffering and fighting for a new page. I encountered the fact of how toxic she was, I might quickly conclude that she lies beyond selfishness and she thought that she had so much, beyond the self-indulgent. And she is merely an abandoned cynical waster girl that she has a huge lack of devotion. I surely needed to eventually wake up and get this devil out of my life.

I no longer could stay patient and suffer more. I planned the next thing to do, was visit the Renaissance Hotel and speak to Darwin to dig deeper to the bottom of all this. I arrived at the hotel around 2pm. I asked the front desk whether I could see Darwin. The man at the concierge seemed a little confused, he had the same reaction as Cherry when I did confront her at the door, then he asked with a voice full of fumble "Why?" However, I kept quiet whilst looking at him with my glaring eyes. The fury and the volcano I felt inside me was because of Darwin and not the attitude of the boy at the front desk. He did not ask any other questions, as he instinctively went into the back office behind the front desk. After about five-minutes, he arrived back with Darwin. This boy was handsome and "Mayabang" which is Tagalog for showoff young boy.

We sat in private, as he started sweating automatically as I felt his heartbeats getting so fast, and when I questioned the boy, he predictably denied all, as he told so many lies himself because that was too obvious and only his heartbeats disclosed everything. Inexpungeable, the idea came to my mind from the bottom of my anger that I should have punched his pretty head, even I was advised I could have killed him and I would not be charged as Adultery was a serious offense in the Philippines, as there is a strict Catholic rule, and this is not tolerated. Therefore, husbands were able to kill anyone having sex with their wives without any criminal charges being laid by the police. Nevertheless, I did not go down this track. Even if some of my Filipino friends insisted that I must kill him, but I'm surely not a murderer. I warned him to keep away from my wife, so I let him leave even he completely denied it! But it was clearly obvious he was her boyfriend.

After seeing this frivolous addict looking boy, I then met with Ruby and I gave her some money to return home and bought her a ferry ticket back to Bohol. She told me almost everything about my evil wife. This young girl was telling the truth, as she was an innocent young girl, and doubt she even knew how to tell lies. I never even bothered seeing Cherry again, as perhaps I would have done something to her or damaged her pretty face.

I just returned to Cebu. My precious boy Geoff needed his dad around, even though he was only three years old, he showed me so much love that I'm grateful for, to have Geoff my son beside me was utterly a bliss, full of love and a very happy little boy with a lovely smile. He became too happy when I'm with him, showing me all his heroes (toys), telling me with his funny words about every idea that came across his mind. I was truly happy my little boy started wondering about life. I'm proud of him as to see him growing up in front of my eyes with all his beautiful details that he has.

Cherry arrived home in time for the Holy Week or Easter as it is known in the world. On arrival, she acted differently as if nothing had happened. That makes me feel sort of stigma instead of she must feel it. This girl! was far too overconfident with her lies, deceit and had no fear of me, as she thought I would tolerate all this forever and just keep paying for her lifestyle. Whilst we were having dinner, she announced that her grandparents were not well at all. I then agreed for her to go to Loay Bohol where her grandparents live so they can visit them. She took Geoff with her and the two maids went with them also. I was totally happy to be alone and take a rest from all these hardships as I was renovating and decorating my Penthouse.

Time went rapidly, and they all arrived back after five days on their supposed mercy visit to her grandparents. One of the maids almost immediately came to my room and told me that Cherry had a boyfriend named Darwin. He and Cherry went to Dipolog, a nearby city from Bohol, and never went to Loay to visit her grandparents, only the two maids and my dear son Geoff stayed in Loay.

The deeds of this evil woman were now truly tiring me until I cannot bear her vulgarity anymore. I rigorously confronted Cherry this time and I asked her in a low voice "Do you know a boy named Darwin?". Then she went too hysterical, and then she started hitting me in the face with a wall clock. Immediately she packed her bags then she left the condo yelling in a sharp way "How dare you accuse me of cheating!"- what a ridiculous joke, and the way how she was acting you can give her an Oscar for that without any doubt! a mask with thousands of faces! She wore them each time so she could pretend. Cherry was so guilty.

I let her leave with the two maids, and of course, my son Geoff would stay here with me. This mind-bending torturous heart-wrenching relationship was finally over. Although, I imagine in her mind that I would beg her to come back. All I have to say is there is no range of chance this woman would ever be part of my life again. Enough is enough, even for super tolerant me. I later learned that Cherry and

Darwin were living in one of the bridal boutiques. I started being careless as our marriage was over a long time ago. I lived alone with my lovely son for several weeks, until I hired a mature lady that was recommended by my friend, to be my new maid. Therefore, I could go to Hong Kong for business soon. She also brought with her a younger girl which was only eighteen-years-old. She said she is her cousin. The girl was pretty with a beautiful smile and long hair, and she has the looks of sweet innocent beauty.

We all lived now in peaceful harmony. And every morning at 6am the young eighteen-year-old girl would deliver me a morning cup of tea with her pretty smiling face and lovely dark eyes, and she stayed in my bed for one hour. It was a very good start to my days. I am a man and no way I could resist what this young girl was offering. After all, in the Philippines, Adultery was a law only for women and did not count for men so I was not breaking the law in any way. I never heard from Cherry which was good.

After a month with the two new maids, I decided to leave for Hong Kong. I surely knew my son would be in safe and good hands while I would be away. The two ladies and my son were now all organized. Geoff and the ladies all were very happy. I now felt it would be no problem to leave and work on my business in Hong Kong.

Chapter 21

HONG KONG.

I trusted the ladies with my precious son and assured myself too that he is in safe hands. I could now focus on my business. I arrived in Hong Kong on a cold Tuesday afternoon with clouds filling up the skies of the city, with the sun barely visible I noticed many eagles circling the outer perimeters of Hong Kong. It was bleak weather on my first day here. The city was full of buildings, people, traffic. Hong Kong was a very crowded city but everything was in harmony, how people walked, how city lights gave the vibes for the atmosphere. I checked into the Wharney Hotel which was decorated with warm colours that gave the feeling of being home.

The hotel was in Lockhart Road in the middle of Wan Chai. This area is renowned for bars with great Filipino bands playing good music. My first night I was out having fun, enjoying a drink with good music, with good spirited people in this place, all cheering with the entertainment. This area has many prostitutes walking in the streets and I was gazing at each one. A lot of them were also in the bars and approached me asking boldly "Can you buy me a drink?". Following my refusal, they then said "Kuripot" which was Tagalog that meant I was stingy. As most of these places gave commissions to the girls for the drinks that customers would buy for them. They were all out of luck with me. All I wanted is to be alone, as I wasn't in the mood for female company. Also, I needed to focus as I had a long busy day planned for the next day so I was in bed by midnight.

After having the long busy day that seemed endless to me, but eventually, night came. My plan tonight was to go along to Happy Valley which was a famous racetrack in Hong Kong. Every Wednesday in the racing season, there was night racing under lights. Happy Valley was fully crowded and loud with many different kinds of people, surrounded by high buildings and bright lights. I felt everything was alive which gave me enthusiasm in an indirect way. Locals loved the excitement that this place gave to all racegoers and gamblers alike. At the track, I caught up with Ronnie, an old Jockey friend of mine that I knew from the times in Australia when I owned racehorses. He was refused a license to ride in Hong Kong, but still he rode track work and did some work for different illegal bookmaking operations helping them field the odds of horses and some inside information that he had from his riding days giving him a living.

Those kinds of men always give you the naughty side of your life that you've missed, they give you another meaning of life far away from a happy quiet life, far away from drama and tragedy, they just take the ride, and they keep riding it until the end, never caring what are the consequences. They just face life with a cigarette or maybe a beer, and if life starts being harsh for them, they take a glass of whiskey, gazing at the whole world like nothing was happening. And more for that, at that night race meeting, I met Paul who is a friend of my jockey friend Ronnie. Paul was a big gambler, impetuous, and rebellious man. Later that year he was picked up at Sydney Airport with abundant quantities of Ecstasy hidden inside wine bottles. I learned later that Paul served ten years for this crime. So, it was an interesting night and my company was also interesting.

Sunday came around so quickly, and this was the day in Hong Kong I looked forward to, as on Sundays the domestic helpers mostly from Indonesia and Philippines were out and about. There were hundreds of them and many of these were too pretty and naughty young girls. I had a contact from my previous visit to Hong Kong where I met a liberated domestic helper. Seeing as this was maybe my last Sunday in this place, she was excited to meet up with me. I spent the day drinking with this young Indonesian girl. She was pretty with almost scarlet lipstick and black hair matching with her eyebrows, her face had a good complexion. She was a good talker, mesmerizing me with every word coming out from her lips. Also, her friend was just like her with genuine simplicity and modesty. As for me I was just drinking and deflating almost everything inside my mind.

The day was a memorable one which I needed to get a smile on my face. That smile which I missed, that smile that had not been there for many months. These young girls were simple as I said, as they were dedicating their lives to work for their families back home in Indonesia which was the culture in these third world countries. However, we danced, we drank and we enjoyed our time like there was no tomorrow. Besides, why should I care about tomorrow? they said that you should be generous for the present moment to have the future, and here I am enjoying it to the fullest. As the girl's curfew was 8pm, I bid them both with a warm farewell and I went to sleep off the pain in my legs and the alcohol which I consumed like there was no tomorrow.

By the following week, I noticed things started to change in Hong Kong. The news had spread around that there was an outbreak of a virus with the name of SARS, that's how they named it, which was short for Severe Acute Respiratory Syndrome. This was an acute respiratory illness caused by

Coronavirus, characterized by fever, coughing, breathing difficulty followed by pneumonia.

I did not know really what it is all about, even almost everything changed in a flash. Hong Kong, where yesterday everything was beating in a magnificent rhythm, but now everything in this city started being debased. I had the notion it was too serious by the fact that Hong Kong was being closed down. All bars and restaurants were completely closed to avoid the spread of this SARS into the greater community. This Coronavirus had the same aura as if an alien had invaded the planet or at least Hong Kong. I wasn't expecting that such a circumstance would flow like this, so I started re-thinking this city, this time and this small island was not a place that I should be. With everything closing down, temperature checks, hand sanitizer, and general panic in the city, I knew it was the right time to leave and go back to the Philippines.

I was able to get out with a direct two and a half Cathay Pacific flight to Cebu. On arrival there were a lot of barricades erected, clung each one tightly to the next as they drew a direct path to the waiting guards, doctors, and nurses. All of them were wearing masks like they were welcoming me at the airport but they were checking each passenger on arrival from Hong Kong. The Hong Kong weather was cold also the plane with the air-conditioning far too high that I seemed to have caught a cold. I was stopped as I had flu symptoms as well for my temperature was a little high. I was immediately taken away in a white van to a hospital and put in a quarantine room with a guard at the front of the door with a gun. I felt like I was a prisoner who committed a cruel crime, they were treating me in a wholly careful manner. Only then did I have a full realization that SARS was a very serious and contagious virus.

I was tested for two days but to my relief, I was cleared to leave and did not have this killer Coronavirus, just a very bad cold. On my release from the hospital, I went and stayed at the Marriott Hotel for the next three days. The hotel was very hospitable, clean and colourful, with everything in the right place with a fabulous design. The room was very comfortable with a nice view over the swimming pool. However, my mind was with my son to see him soon and get back home as soon as I would be totally recovered from the cold. I rested in my room, ordering room service until I was fully recovered as I did not want to spread my cold to my son or maids.

Once I went back to my condo, I just continued living life as normal. Playing golf, enjoying my precious son, as well as the beautiful morning cups of tea from the young girl and all that I had grown to love about Cebu. Although, I could not stay here like this forever and my holiday times have to end for now. My plans to do the business test market in London were already put back two months. So now, it was time to push through with my London plans.

Chapter 22

LONDON AND PARIS.

The time was now right for me to leave for London, as I knew my son Geoff would be in good hands. I already trusted the new maids, because the last time when I was in Hong Kong, they took very good care of Geoff. The two ladies and my son were all organized. Everything was good, and my son and the ladies were very contented. I was now very organized to leave and pursue my business in London.

The day for my departure was now here. The time flies so fast, as we do not notice how possibly could this time flying occurrence happen. Without caring for the things surrounding us until one day you get a smack on your face that wakes you up and you start realizing how much time is precious. I'm here now wasting no time and focusing on my life, my business and my dear son Geoff. Before leaving, I enjoyed a cup of sweet tea on a beautiful morning, sipping my tea slowly with pleasure and calmness, as with other treats that my eighteen-year-old maid gave me.

I left my house with a trust and a good feeling that my son is safe with them. I arrived at Cebu Mactan Airport and the process was very normal. I checked in for my flight without any trouble or obstacles. The first leg was a two-hour flight from Cebu Mactan Airport to Hong Kong with Cathay Pacific, then after a stopover in Hong Kong which I spent in the Qantas Club drinking some complimentary French champagne which now had me primed me for the next leg of my journey. After three hours of transit, I finally boarded a British Airways 747 plane with another thirteen-hours flying time to endure to London.

It was a long trip ahead, and I did not want to think of the distance or the flight time. I settled back into my chair and got prepared for what was ahead. I would have to say the service onboard the British Airways flight was good, but the attitude of the waitresses was firmly not good. Perhaps in hindsight, they could see I had a few too many to drink at Hong Kong. I assumed that was partly my fault that they seemed to have an attitude towards me. I did nothing wrong except, I was a little talkative, a little overly happy with a big excited smile on my face. Anyway, with saying a few extra pleases and thank you I was able to get my fill of red wine. So, after two movies on board, I was totally unconscious, snoring and I did not wake up until breakfast with only three hours left from my destination which was Heathrow Airport London. Who needs sleeping tablets when wine does the trick or did they put sleeping tablets in the wine? A thought but of course that surely was not the case, even though my smiling face was wearing thin on them before I slept the flight away.

Finally, we touched down smoothly at about 6am London time at Heathrow Airport. Although my trip was tiring, I was excited about the new adventure and also, I was very curious about London and this country altogether. This, made me forget about the waitresses onboard or even the long hours in flight where I watched two movies. I had an excited smile on my face as I entered from a large gate leading me directly to the immigration office. I spent a little extra time with the immigration officer who was intensely questioning me with a sharp and hard manner, making it difficult to understand him as I was not used to his British accent at this time. I survived all his questions with my tired eyes now relieved and then eventually my passport was stamped with the officer's smile saying "Welcome to the U.K." I took my passport with my tired face, so now I was free to enter London.

I was very excited to see and to discover this city, remembering an old saying which states "If you are tired of London, then you are tired of life". Of course, I did not tell the immigration officer I was planning to start a business in London, as I only had a tourist visa. Then, I headed up to take my suitcase after standing in my place waiting for it to appear. Here is my suitcase, I took it with an exhausted body. All I wanted for now, was to have a rest from this long trip. I bought a ticket for a door-to-door bus service, and next thing after several stops for other passengers, my bus finally arrived at 8am at my hotel.

My hotel was a bit of an exaggeration which was located in Piccadilly Circus above an Irish Pub, the hotel was surrounded by aesthetic old buildings very different compared to Hong Kong. Everything was completely different in this country, which you can see different people, you can see monuments with a red bus passing by, you can see classic period merged with modernity like buildings with a modern station or just like an aesthetic architect with an advertising screen. I entered my room and it was very small, consisting of a single bed, a sink with the toilet, and a shower outside down the hallway. This would be my home for the next month. I did not mind, because I was only focusing on my goals, as all I needed was a place where I could stay to sleep freely without any other commitments. I was exhausted. After a hot shower, I slept so jetlagged with a hangover from 3pm until the following morning.

Next morning, I left my hotel room or as I now call it my dungeon. I felt being inside my dungeon which was very small gave me a claustrophobic feel, it was cold and dark barely allowing any light to break into my room. Also, London was very bleak, the sky full of clouds and the weather was cold, as it was drizzling rain. This was London weather just as I expected. As time passed over the weeks, I rapidly became accustomed to the weather and actually started enjoying the constant drizzle. However, my first job was to purchase a good elegant umbrella or brolly as they called it in London and keep it always with me.

The time came now to get organized. I rented a shared office in Regent Street which was nearby my residence or dungeon as I called it. I found a printer to print all my stationary, and I was preparing to mail five-thousand letters as a business direct mail test market. I had also bought the leads and had them put on my laptop before I left Australia, I also had my U.K. website up and running. It was now the perfect time to get to work and see what prospects it would bring me.

Following a very full busy and successful day, I decided to explore this city and what is inside her walls. I wanted to reward myself, so I went downstairs to this Irish pub where they had of course Irish whiskey and an Irish band playing underground music. After a few pints of Guinness, I started dancing with the locals and yelling out loud with music playing, like trying to forget everything. I felt everyone has his things to forget, everyone wanted to forget something that happened in his life. I just kept dancing, dancing and dancing. The band finished at about 11pm. I then went for a stroll down to explore the notorious Soho which was the famous red-light district of London which was a fifteen-minute walk from Piccadilly Circus.

This famous Soho district was an interesting place with sex shops, brothels, and bars, gay and lesbian mostly with a few normal pubs mixed in. Neon lights were in every street corner, which was so attractive to visit each place and to get curious about each corner of this district. Soho was very quiet and noisy at the same time, was very sad and happy, very tragic and dramatic at the same time. I wanted to discover more places but the time was late, besides I was too tired so I decided to go back to my hotel. I did not stop anywhere this trip, but I would return another day to explore more again in a future time.

I started walking back to my hotel, carrying my fatigued body in this grey weather and when I was almost home, I glimpsed at a sexy dark-skinned girl with my tired eyes across the street walking the other way. I said "Hi, which is the way Piccadilly?" and she replied without answering my question and only said "You have an accent!" I admitted I was an Australian so seeing as she seemed friendly. I walked across the road and I introduced myself to her politely and she said her name was Jessica, half Brazilian and half Kenyan girl. She had a little unit nearby where she lived with her mother and her sister. Jessica was a friendly girl about five-feet-three-inches tall slim with every perfect detail of her body and the colour of her skin was brightening with her little smile at her beautiful face.

Everything about this girl looked mamamia! as she had a sexy arse that I wanted to touch, but I refrained. I was mesmerized by her simple beauty, long hair braided with the colour of her perfectly shaped face with a small nose and with lips that formed a heart. As well as her London accent, we talked far too long and hit it off well even though I forgot that I was tired and I should go back to my hotel. As I forgot about the Soho district and other happenings, I just enjoyed our conversation. Jessica was a very intelligent lady, as she had a high education standard having previously attended Cambridge University in London. I arranged to meet her for lunch the next day and I had no idea that this girl was almost as crazy as me and my London trip would become more memorable in many ways because of this crazy girl.

The next day I met Jessica at Carnaby Street for lunch at a nice delightful Spanish restaurant, which she confessed later was her favorite type of food. She said she spent a lot of time in Spain and had a close girlfriend living there in Barcelona. We talked about many things and this girl was very worldly. I was enjoying her stories, gazing at her beautiful face and the way she was talking with a glowing smile after each word. After lunch, Jessica drove me to my printer and I picked up my envelopes and letters and dropped them at my Regent Street office. I then made an arrangement on Friday for Jessica and her sister to help me envelope my test market-ready for postage.

It was Wednesday, when I decided it was time to get my fitness back on track. Therefore, I joined the health club at the Marriott Hotel at Marble Arch which was a well-organized and clean health club with very modern fitness machines and good staff, also it was only a twenty-minute tube ride and a further ten-minute walk from my little dungeon above the Irish pub in Piccadilly Circus. I then spent my next day seeing London with her historical places, her heritage, and monuments. There were many tourist attractions. The best way to see them was onboard the famous hop on and hop off red open-air bus to see the sights of the city and enjoy the London breeze. It was a great day touring around and my favorite stops were the Tower of London which was located on the bank of the River Thames with every corner telling a story from history with a hip-knob brighten above the sky with the flag of U.K. dancing with the breeze surrounded by trees. I spent some time at the Notting Hill Markets which was made famous by the movie starring Hugh Grant and Julia Roberts of the same name.

The same night, I was able to get a good seat to see the Miss Saigon Musical at the West End Theatre called Royal Drury. This place was small but wonderful with a perfect architect that takes you to the Renaissance period, as for the show it was magnificent and brought tears to my eyes.

After a good tight sleep, Friday morning had arrived. I got ready to head toward my office where Jessica and her sister Susan were already at the office ready for our three days of work enveloping letters. We all worked hard, even though it was a boring job we were all enjoying the task with lots of laughter and jokes, enjoying the time while working with a good amusement with these two ladies. On the Friday late afternoon, Jessica surprised me with her friend Camilla, who had just arrived at the office from Barcelona, as she was in London for the weekend. They both looked extremely happy to see each other. I could say by the way they embraced and kissed, as when Jessica said she had a girlfriend in Spain, I did not realize they were also lovers. Well, at least that is how it looked to an open-minded person such as myself.

I was looking at Camilla with wide opened eyes without blinking, gazing at this wild Spanish beauty, with her silky hair and long neck. She seemed to have money. She was dressed elegantly in a long red designer dress with her high couture suitable to fashion that was down to her ankles - reminded me of the movie "Lady in Red". She was also holding a Louis Vuitton handbag with her soft hands. She was staying at a five-star hotel in Cromwell Road. Camilla was very slim like a model and five-feet-eight-inches tall. I knew this, as she was taller than me especially with her matching bright red high-heeled shoes. I felt a bit like a young excited boy standing next to this Spanish beauty. I was attracted to her but felt perhaps she was totally out of my class, but she was a warm lady with a cheerful smile on her lovely face and an elegant look that made me feel very comfortable, she was also talking full of contentment with great pleasure and I imagined she was being suggestive.

Camilla and I hit it off well and I even got a hug with her soft arms around me, and a little hot kiss, but not as passionate as the one she gave to Jessica. I was really overwhelmed; I then felt excitement when she invited me to join her and Jessica for a drink that night at her hotel. That night, Camilla and Jessica welcomed me with love and sincere smiles, and soon we began drinking a French champagne. We were laughing, enjoying every second of this beautiful night and these two girls were entertaining and fun. This is how it was for the whole weekend. I was extremely happy to sleep together with these two naughty ladies, as we lived out all the fantasies that anyone could imagine licking, kissing, and erotic naughty sex for two days. They shared me like I was a toy and I felt like I was a Roman Prince sinking into the hedonistic world with these two angels. I fitted into their sex games like we had known each other for years. I never left until Monday morning with Jessica, as Camilla was returning home to Barcelona.

After that amazing weekend, I and Jessica who I had come to realize was bisexual became close, and quite often Jessica would stay in my little room, sometimes an extra girl who Jessica picked up at the Irish pub would also stay over with us. I felt like a Prince who was sent east to find a pearl, and when he arrived the people passed him a cup and the Prince fell into a deep sleep. So, I was like this Prince but in Europe with beautiful ladies. I never complained. We did many things - then all crazy and fantasy dreams that were actually true, as I did not want to wake from this sweet dream. Easter weekend was coming up in London. I and Jessica had arranged a return flight to Paris for Easter staying at Pigalle which I came to discover was the red-light district of Paris.

When we arrived in Paris, the flight was quite comfortable especially with a company like Jessica who was entertaining me with her funny stories and her smile which cannot leave her lovely face. We checked in a hotel which was nearby to the famous Moulin Rouge. The feeling was totally different from London with new people, new culture, new language. Our night in Paris was very calm, but the second night we visited the Moulin Rouge to see Can-Can dancing which was an exciting spectacular performance by sexy long-legged French ladies, with their colourful skirts and the matching shoes dancing in one rhythm like butterflies with beautiful lights and decors, as well as for the vibes that had everyone clapping and whistling. After the show, we went to a little club nearby. It did not take too long before Jessica had found a sweet girl on the dance floor and we were all drinking, and being naughty and really getting carried away at our table when a tap on my shoulder from the security guard came as a surprise and advised us to get our things and were all asked politely to leave for sexual indiscretions inside the club. We all left without saying a word. Although I have to say I was a little embarrassed. The three of us continued back to the hotel, which was called the Timhotel which is also close to Montmartre.

I had now etched a memory of a great time we had in Paris, seeing all the tourist spots like the Eiffel Tower, Notre-Dame, and the Louvre Museum. As I started being hypersensitive for leaving this poetic city full of love and passion, as I never wanted to leave but all things have an ending. I should now return to London and continue my business which I now had the motivation to make my business successful. I had to go back to London to finalize my business after all that was why I was really in London.

My life at this moment was great. I was getting fit, riding the tube and drinking pints in pubs with the friendly locals.

I experienced almost every sexual fantasy a man could imagine. I truly never wanted to leave this exciting ancient city full of amazing history and culture, great civilization, and traditions that one could imagine were possible though I missed my little boy Geoff, and I think he needed me in the Philippines. Sadly, I bided Jessica farewell with a tight hug and a kiss on the cheek. I boarded the Heathrow Express Train from Paddington station to catch my plane and the long journey back to Cebu.

On my flight home, I reminisced about the London business, my test market which had a good sign for the future, and also for the great time that I did spend in London and Paris with great enjoyment and pleasure with Jessica. All these things passed by my mind gently with a proud smile on my face. I hoped to return as soon as possible to do some crazy things again.

I was not home long in Cebu when Jessica called me and told me that she had been diagnosed with cervical cancer, and she sent me photos of her bald head from losing all her hair from the chemo treatment. She was in good spirits. I wished I could return to London to support her, but sadly this was not possible for now.

Chapter 23

LIFE IN CEBU AND MY ARREST.

No matter how far or how long you travel, you would still definitely return home eventually. It was such a great relief to be now home again from my memorable London business trip. And what a grace when a home is my little family, my precious little boy. Geoff was very happy to see Daddy again. I brought him some "Pasalubong" meaning souvenir gifts from London and Paris. He was always asking the maids about me, and for me too, I had been calling him from time to time, as he was always on my mind with his small details, his happy smile. I hugged him so tight and I decided the next two weeks I would give all my time only to him.

We went swimming, trying new games, and playing in parks, I picked places to eat lunch outside and bought his favorite food and drinks. We were both happy and enjoying our time to the fullest as a father and son and more like a friend with a friend. Moreover, my happy days always began with a nice cup of tea each morning. I did miss my pretty tea maker when I was away.

After two weeks of being home, I then contacted my Japanese friend Yoko who said she was so happy I was back home and she convinced me to play golf the next day. There was just me and her this time playing golf, as the Korean lady was away back in Seoul. After a long game, Yoko was the winner, she was a good golf player. We had a nice game of golf and after our game the night was already here. I gave Yoko a ride to her home and upon arrival I parked in front of her house.

I was about to say goodbye and before I got the words from my lips, I was totally surprised when she gave me a big hot kiss on the lips. Her lips were so sweet like a taste of strawberry. We kept kissing and I could not get enough from her lips. And soon, her seat was then slid backward. Yoko then told me gently with her pretty eyes to sit in the passenger's seat, as she kneeled onto the floor and unzipped my pants slowly with her soft hands. Then she started giving me a good suck with her warm eager mouth until I was hard, and the way how she did it was like she was sucking something made of 24-carat gold. It seemed like it was her first time to do this but this lady was thirty-five years old and was previously married, so surely not.

She then pulled down her panties and I felt a nice temperature in her body and soft skin, she then put her panties on my face and my smile, with her hands on my chest. What a beautiful aroma they were. Her panties were pink in colour and so wet. Yoko then sat on top of me on the passenger's seat, as she slid on top of me until I was now inside her. She started moving slowly with her nice body, my hands on her waist, as she was holding me with her arms and my head was on her breasts breathing her aroma and hearing her moaning. She was so wet and the noise she made was too loud, I had to put her panties in her mouth before someone heard her. Yoko was very horny and hungry for sex and her eyes were showing her enjoyment. I was about to climax and she went back onto the floor and swallowed every drop with some coming out the side of her mouth. This experience was just perfect exciting sex we had and Yoko later admitted it was her first time in years to have sex and told me her only other encounter was with her husband but he climaxed so quick, she never had time to climax.

After this encounter which was utterly unexpected but unforgettable, life became exciting and amazing. As all I did was played golf and have sex with this Japanese lady in the car, in toilets, restaurants, movie theatres, and virtually everywhere and every chance we had as if we were just hot teenagers.

Soon the Korean lady returned from Seoul and once again, the three of us played golf. I noticed the Korean lady was not happy at all. She seemed jealous, as I think she knew what was going on with me and Yoko. Even though we were so discreet. Well, I thought we were, but perhaps no! Nevertheless, the eyes would always tell a story. Now Yoko started taking care of herself more, dressed so well with a stunning look, even she put on makeup and French perfume not like before. She had become a very happy adventurous lady and a very sweet caring person, much more than she was previously.

Life was exciting, happy, and good. I had not a worry in the world. But things do not always go as you expect them to, especially when you have a lot of joy and positive things around you. Good family, good health, good memories and moments. In such a period life would bring you Fall instead of Summer. That's how from nowhere to all of a sudden, things were about to change and I would be soon looking at the other side of life.

A sudden surprise came after not hearing from Cherry for at least one year. She called me, and she said that she wanted to meet in SM Mall at Starbucks to talk. I had no idea about what we should talk about. Everything was over between me and her, nothing left to talk about. Things did not add up and against my better judgement I reluctantly agreed, I wanted to tell her we were already divorced as I filed in Australia. Cherry was already an Australian permanent resident and my son was an Australian citizen. Furthermore,

I had been having a plan to give her a $100,000 Australian dollars settlement even though she did not deserve one dollar. I thought this would settle everything and we could both move on. However, this serpent still wanted to spread her venom into my life, she did not get enough of what she already did. She wanted to sway my life with her chains, her poison was volatile, as she started being intolerable.

I arrived at SM Mall and entered Starbucks. I saw her at the first step at the Starbucks door, she was sitting alone. This woman never changed; she stayed the same. She became like an old witch casting her black magic spells, moreover, this old witch was extremely agitated. I proceeded to sit next to her, and suddenly she ran away. I did not understand what was happening until five police officers ran to me like it was a movie and I was an escaped prisoner. I had no chance to run, I got arrested with handcuffs on both hands with the voice of the officer saying "You are charged with Habeas Corpus".

I realized after my arrest, Cherry was playing her game behind my back, with another knife on my back. I am still alive. That was too obvious a corrupt arrest warrant that was issued and meant I kidnapped my son and I have to return him. Lies of course! However, I fell into the devil's trap and now I had a big problem and was thrown in the nearby Mabolo police station lockup close to SM with at least twenty others Filipinos inside the same cell as me.

Chapter 24

JAIL.

It had been like a nightmare, I wanted only to get up from this bad dream. Unfortunately, it had been the reality. A reality which I fell into with my good intention to talk with Cherry calmly as I said to offer her a settlement. However, it ended like this with handcuffs on my hands. The police drove me to the Mabolo Police lockup and at the front of the police station were news reporters and cameras waving in my face like I was a Hollywood actor or in this state. I felt like I did a cruel crime, which I was still surprised how hastily life changed in just a few seconds with the tricky game of the devil Cherry. She smiled with a wily smile on her cunning face, as she put on a big acting performance like a Hollywood actress worthy of an award. She was off her face on drugs which was noticeable by everyone. I was taken to the lockup at the back of the station, as the handcuffs eventually were freed from my aching wrists.

Once I was inside, I started receiving abundant texts on my phone that I would be dead by morning. However, I guess this was all part of the game. I was completely in a bad mood now and sitting in this grubby lockup room on the concrete floor. The little tiny room had bars and was too small with twenty people also locked up with me. This place even the rats would not live here, and the level of degeneration was very low, it was like hell for me, but maybe salvation for others. There were no beds, no chairs, and just a smelly toilet in the room. This room was very hot and full of humidity and full of the bad smell of people's breaths. Everything was obnoxious and this room was merely for me an infernal abyss and only fit for the people who are like Cherry. One of the Filipino prisoners took an instant dislike to me and attacked me swinging punches. I was lucky I could defend myself, as this man was maybe on drugs and could not fight, maybe he was also put in there to scare me. Nevertheless, I called the Australian Embassy and told them my story that I was arrested with no charges and no bail, but they were disinterested and ended the call by just hanging up on me. I was now on my own.

Several hours had passed while sitting in this room full of dirty prisoners, as everyone started being quiet, even the one who attacked me. They were sitting on the floor waiting for something! something that they do not know, maybe their salvation? maybe their punishment. I was feeling very low and very stupid that I was in a such position like this. However, at the end of the day, there was no point dwelling, as I had to act fast. I reluctantly decided to call my old friend Vic Diaz's house who was now not a well man and bedridden after a stroke a few months earlier. His son Carlos answered the phone and gave me the number of Vic's nephew who was a lawyer, as I did not want to bother my friend Vic as he had enough problems simply fighting for his life. I called Butch his nephew. When he heard my story, he became angry at what was happening and also sounded embarrassed that his country would do such a thing as this to a foreign visitor. He sent a lawyer friend of his from Cebu to see me in the lockup. He advised me the only way I could get out was to surrender my precious son whom I refused. After all, his mother was a drug addict, also she was involved with big-time drug dealers. Her associates consisted of high-profile drug dealers one of which was the Mayor and also a very rich business man in Cebu and his partner Heather, who was the president of a bank in Cebu and laundered all the drug money for a wealthy Cebu businessman who was the number one drug lord in the city.

I spent a whole week in jail and I figured out that I had no alternative but to surrender my son. I felt so angry at this woman. How could she look after Geoff with her drug addiction? with her debased life and insecure mind, as she has a huge lack of devotion, how could this drug-addicted woman take care of herself? and she wanted to take care of Geoff. There was so much absurdity in these facts which was too obvious to everyone. We did appeal to the court but the judge was undoubtedly bribed by these evil people and his only words were "The mother has the kid now so get out of here! maybe return to Australia would be a good idea". He refused to even to listen to the whole facts, to the real personality of this devil woman and how much I would fight for my son, but without any logical reasons, they took my precious son away.

My experience in jail was not too bad besides the man who attacked me, the smell of the room and the first horrific night sleeping with an eye open and my nose covered from the bad stench of sweating prisoners who maybe had not bathed for weeks, also a backache from the hard cold concrete floor. However, the police chief was a good man, as he knew what was really going on. Each night we would drive up to the restaurant with two other officers to have a few drinks and eat nice food. I spent most of the days in the Police Chief's office drinking with him and the other officers. These officers who now seemed to be my friend, maybe because of my treats I gave them, all insisted on killing my ex-wife Cherry. Of course, I did not accept that offer, as I felt that would be just a setup. I do not murder people, even though for a brief period of time I did contemplate the idea.

Finally, I was out. I headed directly to my condo at City Lights, and all I wanted to do was stay alone for a period of time. I decided to send the two maids to their province, although those beautiful mornings would no longer exist, I no longer trusted anyone now in Cebu. I needed just to disappear and be out of the view of people. I then went to Manila and stayed in the Hyatt Hotel for a week, not at my condo in Makati palace. After that, I contacted a Fiscal friend of mine from the Makati court building. A Fiscal in the Philippines is likened to a District Attorney in places like America. His name was Attorney Price which was coincidental as I had to pay the price with money that needed to be paid to shortcut an arrest warrant for Cherry and her addict boyfriend Darwin. I filed an Adultery case against my wife with the Makati Fiscal's Office and also with the help of my lawyer from Cebu who was now here in Manila helping with all the paperwork.

Patiently, I waited in Manila for her arrest warrant to be processed before travelling back to Cebu for my next court hearing. I gave the arrest warrant before the hearing to my NBI friend Austin who arrested Cherry, he then put her in the NBI lockup. Now, she could feel the cold humidity of the floor and the dirty smell of sweat as I did. With her drug addiction, she will not survive in this cell. This became an amazing drama with her family members screaming and yelling as her mother attacked me. Eventually, she was taken away and I just left the building inconspicuously out the side entrance. The pawn boyfriend Darwin has disappeared like an afraid rat, nowhere to be found.

Cherry now faced a serious criminal charge against her. I had bargaining power as an adultery charge carries a seven-year jail term in the Philippines. Quite fair enough this law was only for women not for men, unless a man slept with a married woman. Now I played my cards my own way as it was, she who started this game not me! I was about to move on but I think she will not get enough to spread her poison until you cut the serpent's head. With another word I ought to stop her from playing games with me. This is how it was now with Cherry and her lawyer filing charge after charge against me. In total five more cases. Whatever, they were all made up and very weak and thrown out quickly with a paid bribe to the Cebu Fiscal's office.

I had now returned to Manila and waited at the Hyatt Hotel again, and just remained calm as all these problems were weighing heavily on my financial and mental being. I felt too tired to bear all these things, I'm just a quiet man who needs a few beers and enjoying the sun or going to the pub. I do not want drama in my life. I just wanted to live free out of this sort of life that I'm having now. Life became so complicated because of an evil drug addict ex-wife who was giving her lawyer fifty percent commission on how much money they could extract from me.

Chapter 25

VANUATU.

I was enjoying my first night at the Hyatt Hotel which was my favorite hotel in Manila with an amazing view, friendly staff and the room was very spacious with a large king-sized bed, beautiful plants inside, and soft lights. I felt that I needed to relax even just a little bit after those harsh days that I had been through. I went to the bar downstairs where there was a good band playing. The music and the fabulous singer gave me a relaxed attitude. I kept listening to the music with a cold San Miguel Beer in my hand enjoying it with the rhythm of the music. Whilst listening, I was enjoying my first beer. I noticed two frizzy-haired men that were also having a beer and looking a little out of place as they say "They looked like fish out of water". I went over to them, as I introduced myself with a sincere smile and my beer in my hand and I inquired with a little curiosity. I was in a good mood to have a nice talk with someone. Especially strangers who actually do not know anything about me. Then I asked "What are you doing in Manila?" They said with a cool voice "We are working for the government in Vanuatu". I understood from them that they were in Manila for a conference.

I and these two fellas hit it off very well. They were really happy and friendly people making a lot of jokes and laughter. These kinds of jovial people always give you tranquility and a good sense of humor towards life, towards things which sometimes you see them harsh. We were having an interesting conversation, as we drank a few more drinks. They admitted that they were very attracted to the Filipina. So, I asked "Would you both like to meet a girl tonight?" As I knew a place where girls for a small fee would spend the night with them. They excitedly said "Yes!" I then replied "Okay! I will take you there later to choose a girl".

We had another two beers and before I knew it, we were off in a taxi to Mabini Street. One of the districts in Manila City where the girls worked. There was a lot of traffic, reflected lights, and a lot of noise filling our ears. With many faces that passed by and neon lights flashing from each place with different girls and sometimes with a bunch of girls wearing the same clothes or the same pattern of a dress like they were creating a brand. The weather was warm and humid with a soft breeze entering from the taxi's window. On arrival, I told the taxi driver to wait for us, then we went inside the club. There was a big window where on the outside you can see the girls, but inside was a mirror that they looked at. The girls could not see outside and about thirty girls were sitting on three levels on bench-like chairs. They all displayed number tags and the two Vanuatu men chose a girl each and paid the money to the Madam.

We were then on our way back to the hotel. I explained to my new friends earlier to give their night companion a little bonus in the morning. The girls must stay the night with them, and in the morning, we would send them back in the hotel car. The reason it must be done this way is there was a lot of corruption in this country, tourists are always a target and they could make up a story that the girls were never returned, or even that you bashed the girls, then the police would come for money. Therefore, they needed proof that they were returned and the Hyatt Hotel cars are trusted drivers. I sat in the front and my two friends were in the back of the taxi with the two girls kissing and cuddling with the biggest smiles I have ever seen on a human face before. On arrival, I bid them goodnight at the hotel entrance and told the girls to treat my friends well and I gave the girls a small cash incentive each also.

The next morning was very warm with sunlight entering my room giving a good feeling with the fresh smell of flowers bringing more joy. I headed downstairs to have a nice breakfast. I saw my two friends there and they were very happy with a big smile on their face and sparkling eyes that they would say something which you cannot describe, showing without words that they had a great night. They thought I was the greatest man in the world for their treats. They treated me like I could walk on water. We all were getting on well. After a few days with my friends, they surprised me with an invitation to return to Vanuatu with them. I never even thought for a minute, as I was needing something to make me alive again, and travel was the only way especially with a new different place, and I was doing nothing much at the time just waiting around. I said, "Why Not!" before I knew it, we were on our way to Brisbane with Qantas overnight and connected with an Air Vanuatu plane the next day. I did not know what to expect, but it seemed like a little adventure that I could not refuse.

I was truly surprised when we arrived at Vanuatu Airport surrounded by coconut trees, where this country was full of nature with clean fresh air to breathe and white clouds scattered across the blue sky. They say here the crabs taste like coconuts as the trees are so plentiful that the crabs break the hard shell and eat the coconut inside, not sure if it was a myth or true. It was a beautiful day and this beautiful day was completed when a big white limousine with flags and Government plates picked us up at the airport with the driver wearing a formal dress and black cap.

We were soon on our way; we were talking about almost everything with jokes and laughter as if we were old friends and we knew each other for a long time. I felt comfortable with them especially when you are with this sort of people. You do not need to prove or to explain yourself, you just be who truly you are.

They dropped me at my hotel-styled resort that they arranged and was told to rest and they would pick me up later. The staff at the hotel treated me like a King, perhaps they thought I was a dignitary when in fact I was only a simple happy-go-lucky Australian here to party with my two newfound friends. I took a long hot shower and then slipped into a luxury bathrobe, then I rested on a luxurious comfortable white bed while looking over a wonderful view. I felt dizzy because of the plane, so I caught a few hours of sleep in a room fit for the King of England.

I was all rested after a good sleep and waiting for my pickup and sure enough, about 6pm a car arrived with my friends inside handing me a cold beer. We were dropped off at a big white government building in the center of town. We went inside to meet some other people. I was just gazing at everything with a fascinated eye like a new world to me. I said nothing, I just followed and was mesmerized by this beautiful adventure. I met two men who were introduced as the Vice Prime Minister and the Minister for Finance. They were just like my friends happy and simple and of course humble without any arrogance. So now with my two friends from Manila, the gardener from the front lawns, the Vice Prime Minister, and some other Ministers, we were off to the pub.

On arrival, at the entrance, we had received a respectful and warm welcome. The party started and we were all thirsty and ready to drink. The pub was very simple with many different people. Everyone was completely having fun to the fullest. It was a memorable night that I could not forget my whole life. These Vanuatu people could drink and we had an amazing time, as we had more laughs and singing the whole night without stopping than I could ever remember in my life. These people were simple-happy with not a care in the world. I felt that I blended in well with them and they treated me like their brother. I really loved Vanuatu and the rest of my stay on this sun-soaked Island was spent enjoying fishing, diving, drinking and dancing where I learned a few of the native dance moves. I truly just had the time of my life with these friendly and humble people. I did not get involved with local girls as maybe they wanted someone serious and that was not me, even though I am sure they would have been fun to be with.

Time flies without perceiving how it went this fast. Sadly, it was now time to depart this magnificent affectionate country and I sincerely did not want to leave, but I had to return to the Philippines to fix my problem there. I bid farewell to my two new friends as I thanked them for this amazing invitation and for this extraordinary experience that I had. Once again, I was sent to the airport in the white limousine with flags flying. I was going to miss this place where there was no class of people and they were all just living in perfect harmony.

I was on the plane and airborne when reality now took over my thoughts. I knew that when I arrived in the Philippines, I had to prepare for my court case which I am sure would be full of my ex-wife's stressful drama.

Chapter 26

MAKATI BURGOS STREET MEETING AND TRAVELS.

I flew from Vanuatu with a heart full of joy but a mind full of disquiet about what was waiting for me in Manila. I changed planes at Brisbane Airport and soon I would be back in Manila after a great holiday with my new amazing worthy friends. Truly! this trip was an unforgettable experience that I would treasure for years to come. It was full of beautiful memories of what I did there, with all the humble people who have such a substantial weight in Vanuatu. With all these things inside my mind, I was also thinking about what would be my plan for now. I decided to stay in my condo in Burgos Street Makati.

I arrived in Makati and my feelings were very heavy with a lot of pressure that I did not know from what source it came from. I also had mixed emotions at the same time. Maybe disappointed, or maybe a little bit sad with the happiness which I had on my trip. It was everything strange in one moment, I kept standing with a heavy breath inside my chest. I then decided to head up to my condo and have a rest.

I was just lying on the bed just starring at the ceiling and contemplating, like my mind was in a race that affected my brain somehow. I felt signs of anxiety creeping up on my mental health. I then escaped this heavy thinking by leaving my condo and went downstairs to a bar near my hotel called the Matrix. The Matrix with its synthesis of red and black colour was very relaxing with beautiful heat that makes me feel quite forsooth. I sat at a table at the front of the bar, close to the street and watch all the pretty girls walk by and enjoying aesthetically watching the happenings in Burgos. Believe me! Plenty was going on as normal in this notorious location. Here I was sipping a San Miguel Beer minding my own business when I noticed two girls looking directly at me which was not usual in Burgos. In this area a lot of foreigners could be found. Where there are foreigners, there are girls looking to catch a husband or a boyfriend. However, most of them were just looking to pick up a little extra money for some naughty things in return or even just a few free drinks and maybe some food. You have to keep in mind this is the Philippines and girls would do almost anything to get some money for their families.

These two girls were very attractive that I could not ignore and were far too much "Tukso" which means temptation in English. I opted to invite these two attractive girls to join me and even from a distance they both saw my wave, so they did not hesitate to come to join me. They introduced themselves with a nice smile on their cute faces. The first girl was named Abby, who was about twenty-five years old and the other one's name was Inna as she said with a little giggle of sweetness. She was extra pretty and she was about eighteen years old. Or sure! I did hope she was eighteen, as she looked very young. I bought them a few drinks and some food and we were all having fun. They added extra joy to my night which helped me forget my problems. With a few drinks and good conversation at the bar, the time went passed very quickly. The night was getting late so I invited them to my condo for some tea or coffee. Although, we all knew what was going to happen when they came to my condo. Even though there was no mention of money which made me realize they had a little class not to discuss money, maybe they did not need money.

Before long they agreed, and with a throb in my pants we walked home together. Once we arrived at my condo, the older one started being a little argumentative which turned me off. The young one started kissing me and then my hands pulled her waist close to me with her thighs and her body then wrapped around me. I kept kissing her passionately and my hands were touching her soft body whilst tasting her sweet lips. I could not stop kissing her. I took off all of her clothes slowly with nice kisses over her body and between her breasts was like a sweet smell of flowers. We made love very sweet for at least an hour. She stayed close to me all night cuddling. While the older one, stayed also in the same bed. I did not touch her, as she acted asleep whereas I enjoyed the fruits of this young girl Inna.

After that night, also the next month or so, we travelled together and I felt like Sultan Suleiman with two wives. Before too long, I was tasting them both each time they stayed with me. I am sure people thought this was a little funny but remember this is the Philippines, and as they say "Only in the Philippines", a well-known expression that meant no one really cared as long as you were happy.

We first travelled up to Angeles City, which was a very crowded city with a lot of motorcycles and people walking randomly with every light flashing from each establishment, and hot girls sitting everywhere, most of them they were wearing short dresses. Every market was crammed with many shoppers. This city was alive! so we stayed for one week. I hung out with some old Australian acquaintances at the Swagman. However, they did not stay for too long, as it seemed they were a little jealous of my happiness and my happy nights with my two wives. Perhaps they thought

I was a showoff, but I was just going with the flow but I did understand their jealousy.

We left Angeles City. We caught a bus down to La Union and stayed at a nice resort there on the beach where I knew nobody. It was more relaxed with these two pretty girls with sunlight touching our skin slightly and the blue beach surrounded by trees. I put sunscreen on the shoulders and the back of the young pretty girls. They gave me a very soothing massage while I was resting and enjoying the beautiful weather. These girls swam every day and liked to dance at night.

Then our next trip was to Baguio, this time in a car. I recollected my last harrowing trip in a bus up the steep mountain. We all enjoyed the cold nights and this place which was full of pine trees and cool weather which gave you the attraction to make another adventure and challenge yourself. But soon returned this time flying back to Manila which was a fifty-minute flight to avoid the eight-hour bus ride. I feared for my life flying out of this mountainous city, as the small propellers of the Asia Spirit plane had a steep climb, and seemed we just missed the top of the mountain peak. Flights were stopped from this airport one month later as an Asia Spirit plane hit the mountain on takeoff killing all thirty-six passengers on board. This news sent a shiver through my spine, but obviously, it was not my time to go yet and I had a lot more stupidity to live before leaving this crazy world.

I arrived in Manila with my two temporary fantasy wives. After all, we were having too much fun and of course enjoying a daydreaming life, with cool moments which I felt the world was mine with these two simple girls. We had an enormous lust for life. Which made me keep in mind that I was still alive above everything else. We stayed at the Manila Hotel and whilst sleeping, the first night about

3am Abby awoke screaming claiming that there was a ghost in the room, which she said was a lady wearing an old-fashioned green dress and said nothing but just put her finger to her lips and gave the gesture "Shhh".

Abby rapidly packed her things shaking, so I sent her home in a hotel taxi. I and Inna stayed together at the hotel for the next week and we never saw any ghosts which was a relief to us both. Most nights we would go down to Malate which is only a fifteen-minute walk and watch some great live music at the Cowboy Grill Bar with good bands playing. The bar was a famous music venue in Manila.

Inna loved to dance with her perfect shape moving slowly with the rhythm of music and her pretty smile looking at me. Although she had no I.D. The security guards accepted a 500 Peso note as a valid I.D. and let her in. Every time we went there, we always went to the front of the line like we were V.I.P, as they loved this I.D. that I gave them. One night, we also went to the Hobbit House and watched the Philippine legend singer Freddie Aguilar. The Hobbit House was Freddie's bar. The waiters and waitresses were all "Pandak" which meant short or midgets' people in English. Freddie Aguilar even though he was getting a little old, still played guitar smoothly with a fabulous voice that made the atmosphere very calm with the rhythm of bass guitar and drums was almost like we were in a concert. He still sang like a true professional, after all, he was known as the Bob Dylan of the Philippines, and to be given that distinction, he had to be so good.

After a great time with Inna, I did not get bored of her existence around me. However, I decided to send her home. As for me, I went back to my little condo in Burgos Street to make future plans and enjoy being alone for a while.

Chapter 27

CEBU COURT HEARING.

I had been enjoying my solitude, after my good times that I spent together dancing, partying, and drinking with the girls especially Inna, who was a very exciting girl. I'm now just living day to day with myself living every moment, enjoying everything that surrounds me, including the Philippine culture starting each morning drinking coconut juice in the shell that I bought from the street vendor and walking to the Renaissance Hotel at Greenbelt, about a twenty-minute walk from my Condo in Burgos Street. I got fit at their gym and swimming pool.

I vividly remember one day when I bought a chicken sandwich from a street vendor and just after one bite, I opened the sandwich which had no taste on my tongue. Weirdly, I saw onion, tomato, and lettuce but no chicken. I kept looking at the lady who made my sandwich and I said with my opened eyes as I lifted my eyebrows wondering about the chicken "There is no chicken!" She simply said with a "Kawawa" or sad eyes in English "Sorry sir! We are out of chicken" so then without any other word, I modestly closed my sandwich. I just ate it without complaining. I just imagined there was chicken in the sandwich. As I was eating for a moment, I started wondering if this was a joke? like I was on Candid Camera or a similar TV show. This is life, sometimes you ought to imagine something fine which is not fine and keep enjoying life, despite the harsh circumstances in an absurd way with quietness.

Time had now passed, with all these beautiful memories with my Vanuatu friends and the two wives. Yes! I did have many things to remember, as they would be always in my mind and now it was time for my court hearing in Cebu. The hearing was critical and seemed a formality and my precious son would be returned to his daddy. I missed my little boy so much as he was happy with me and I always felt proud of this happiness.

Recently, I and my lawyer worked to get this happiness back to my son, as we prepared well. I could get back my son Geoff who I was always worried about, as I had been very bothered to let him be with a devil! That devil surely would not take care of him! instead, she would just take drugs. There was an order, I was not allowed within one-hundred-meters of him and Cherry. I had no chance of seeing him to avoid jail. I and my lawyer had been waiting at Starbucks because we flew early in the morning before our court hearing. We were just sitting with heartbeats for raising hope to get my son. I did not mind the sweet bitterness of coffee as my mind always was with my son Geoff. We stayed just in Starbucks until the time of the hearing.

We arrived at the courthouse. This devil woman was surrounded by her friends and family, with a lot of drama in their eyes which you can see they were thinking how much money would they all get. The hearing went for about three hours and It started with this big liar Cherry making up many lies while she delivered her testimony. She sewed a lot of lies but eventually, she would lose the path where she began. Once, she was cross-examined and we showed documents that she had previously had an abortion and when we brought up the adultery case that was still ongoing, the judge had to stop the cross-examination and take us all into his chambers, as it was not going well for Cherry.

The judge virtually had no choice but to give my son back to me and also give me one-hundred-percent custody. Also, her claims for money, as well as her other claims were utterly denied but for goodwill, I agreed to give her 500,000 Pesos, which she would have to give half of the money to her lawyer.

After all this, everything had been done. I took my precious little boy who is still five years old. I had now planned to dedicate my life to raising this boy and taking care of him. Geoff was the best behaved and happiest kid in the world with his happy smile and his existence in my life was very important to me, as he sounded funny speaking his words. I was just enjoying my little family time with him, going to the park, playing, and doing everything as a father and son. I had agreed to let him have time with his mother, in which I agreed to let him stay with her for three weeks every Christmas.

This game which was started by a devil girl was unnecessary and expensive. However, the end of evil is always like this, always losing, always falling into an abyss. I was about to move on but this girl wanted to play, and I showed her that I can also play this game. I was dealing with a devil with horns and a drug-infected mind. This is how it would happen. Whether you did deal with this sort of demon and her poison was not enough for it to kill me. It just actually gave me more power to face her and put an end to her contagious being in my life.

Just a bit of communication and common sense and all of this would have been avoided. Cherry also would have been 4-Million Pesos richer. This is what happens when dealing with arrogant overconfident people, who are sailing in a big ocean of illusion and lies, of selfishness and a lot of self-indulgence. A physiologist would say this is called Narcistic syndrome.

Chapter 28

BAY GARDENS MANILA AND ANOTHER COURT CASE.

My expensive court cases and drama finally had come to an end. This nightmare which had been directed by a serpent which unsuccessfully attempted to poison me and surrounded me with her evil fangs. Well! At least for now, you can never actually be in peace with a snake around, as you cannot expect when and where this creature would poison you. You just remain anxious and worried. This is, for now, my state! I still had a lot of worries that this was not over and I did not have to be a psychic to think this way.

It was the best choice to make is that I leave Cebu, and that was actually what I had now decided without any hesitation. I reluctantly decided to sell my beautiful Penthouse in City Lights, which I spent all my spare time decorating and renovating with a huge passion and love. I would now move to Manila. I then purchased a two-bedroom condo at a place called Bay Gardens which was close to Mall of Asia, which at the time was the biggest shopping center in South East Asia and the 11th largest mall in the world. The residence was a very beautiful place with a lot of facilities near to me, as well as the area was peaceful and had a fresh sea breeze blowing from Manila Bay, with new people of course who do not know me at all, who were mostly visitors and tourists.

My condominium and the mall were both built on the reclaimed land near Manila Bay in Pasay. I enrolled my son Geoff at San Augustine school in Makati. I then hired a maid to help with the cooking and the cleaning. I felt like I had just started a new life away from everything, I just wanted to be happy and live a simple life with my son. Every morning, the big yellow school bus would pick up my little man at 7am and return him at 5pm from school. I finally got the peace of mind which I had been needing.

My days were totally free and I spent my time chasing naughty girls in Mall of Asia. I was also running my business from home. I sometimes had to travel for business in Singapore, Hong Kong, and every so often to Australia. While I had been away, I always had my maid's sister stay in the condo helping Maria to look after my son Geoff.

My Japanese friend Yoko would occasionally come to visit me in Manila. We would play golf and enjoyed each other's company just like in the previous days when we played in Cebu. Yoko soon moved back to Japan, and she had been staying in Tokyo. After her third invitation, I then decided to visit her in Tokyo. Yoko was a very nice lady, as she showed a lot of affection for me and my son too! She wanted both of us to come and live with her in Tokyo. Sadly, I told her with great sincerity from the bottom of my heart without hurting her feelings that I cannot do this, particularly at this time. I did not want a serious relationship after my disastrous previous marriage. After all, I had become a bit of a playboy, therefore I was not sure if I could dedicate my life to only one woman. I had been tired of that commitment. I only wanted to enjoy my life in peace away from stress and distractions. Nevertheless, we still emailed each other and called for a while, but eventually, this ended and life moved on for me. Although the time that we did spend together was unforgettable with a lot of memories as the first time we kissed in the car and how well she had been playing golf. Even the talks that we used to have were great and Yoko was a very beautiful woman. I remembered the times we had together and I would always remember this wonderful person. However, everything has an ending and this was my ending with Yoko, I set her free.

My life now was free. I enjoyed this freedom with my little man, who started growing up day by day in front of my eyes. We became very close to each other and he had been telling his stories about school and his new friends and how the teacher is so nice and what he did in school. This boy started having stories to tell that made me very proud of him. My maid Maria and Geoff got on well and he was a good sweet boy and a loveable boy always. While in Manila, I would sometimes bring Filipina girls home from the mall and most of these were pretty and very naughty. I was discreet not to let my son see my bad habit of enjoying naughty girls.

At this time, I began to be suspicious of Gary in Singapore, who was my business partner, as the income from the business was down and not much money was being banked until I finally had the business audited. I was very disappointed; Gary had stolen more money than I could even believe possible. I stopped this partnership and planned soon to set up in Singapore on my own.

It was now Easter. I started wondering about the time which flies very fast like thunder! Sometimes, it took a lot of time for bad things to pass and a very short time for good things and good memories! But at the end, you will sit alone and reminisce about all these things, you will figure out that you are proud of yourself, proud of who you are. Geoff was almost eleven years old now, I started to notice that he was growing up very fast. It was holiday time, so I allowed him to visit his mum Cherry in Cebu for ten days.

As every time I dropped him there, she always returned him. So, I agreed.

I had a really bad feeling this time, as my intuition was telling me that something would surely happen. As Cherry was with Heather when I dropped him off and I also had a bad feeling about her. This lady was overconfident because of her wealth, I think she was laundering money for the drug lord in Cebu.

My fears wistfully became reality, when I went back to pick up my son. They were not at home, nowhere to be found, like the earth opened her mouth and swallowed them. They vanished as with my good heart; I was allowing Geoff to visit her with a big kindness to make her see him. However, this devil would not get tired of the tricky games. After a while, she texted that she would not return him and many bad words were contained in her texts. This time, she seemed confident or I do not know! Perhaps she was faking it as always, as she fakes many things. Even though I had full custody, I had to hire a lawyer, who was a friend of Austin my NBI friend. His name was Rodriguez and he wrote for the local newspaper, but still was a registered lawyer. Therefore, he said we could get a court order to return my son.

I continued to wait for almost one month for my day in the court hearing. I could not continue to pass all my time waiting for a court hearing, as I had business to manage. I got a call at 3pm while I was in Singapore on business. The call was that I needed to attend court at 10am the next morning. I had to pay for an expensive ticket to fly early in the morning to Cebu to catch the court hearing. On arrival, I raced as quickly as I could to arrive at the courthouse with virtually five-minutes to spare. I was surprised and felt something was wrong! Inside the court room, there was nobody at the hearing.

I finally tracked down the girl that called me. She was the clerk of the court, and she said with a smart look on her face "The judge was sick, there is no court today!" I replied whilst gasping from my run to be here on time "I just flew from Singapore to be here!" She replied with a big cold smile "Then go back to Singapore". With my wasted energy, time, and the air ticket for the flight, I could have said a lot of things to this woman. I pulled myself together, as I held my anger inside and walked out knowing full well that was just harassment. I had been becoming more and more disillusioned with the law of the Philippines or lack of law to be more precise.

Finally, it had been another month of waiting, like I was suspended waiting for something to set me free. We got a court hearing eventually. Inside the courtroom my son had refused to come anywhere near to me and it was too obvious that this devil Cherry washed his brain, as he became afraid or even closer to terrified of me. He was screaming at the top of his voice. God knows what this evil woman and her mother had done to my son. He was distressed and extremely unhappy, as his eyes were telling something. Like a puzzle that I should solve and he was seemingly filled with absolute total terror.

Although the state of my son, as he was in a totally distorted condition the judge ordered that Cherry return my son to me immediately. Of course, she refused and left the courthouse with mystifying overconfidence with my son. This serpent was not alone, you cannot build all this confidence from nothing! as Only God knows what is inside this witch. After over a week of her declining to return Geoff to his daddy, I had no choice but to file a contempt of court case, as it was my last resort to get my son back as already, I could see the damage to this boy's mind might be irreparable.

These people are all drug people. Heather, Cherry, and the rich drug baron named Charles. Once again, I found myself in a stressful situation. I started becoming so tired of this drama and all these games. In hindsight, I should have never allowed Geoff to visit his mum. But none of this kind of thinking will get my son back. I should act instead of thinking these kinds of thoughts. I had to pursue this contempt of court case which seemed the only chance of getting him back without putting myself in a dangerous situation. I know what drug people are capable of so I kept out of sight until the next court hearing.

By the time we finally went to court, Heather the drug money launderer walked inside the Judge's Chambers just before the hearing and ten-minutes later walked out and said to all the people in the courtroom with big arrogance and self-confident "All is Fixed" which at the time seemed a little confusing. Sure enough, when the Judge walked out and took his place, he said to me and my lawyer the same way the clerk had told me to go back to Singapore with cold words "I have changed the child's custody to the mother so get out of my court!". We endeavored to speak, but the Judge yelled aggressively at my face. I had no chance to even say one word! but to leave. I had been devastated. Obviously, this was illegal for the Judge to do such a thing like this but I was a foreigner and the prejudice against me was very apparent.

I was in total despair, and my inner heart was literally in sorrow for the next week. Before long, I had received a message from my lawyer and he said that the lawyer of Cherry would return my son if I paid $50,000 American dollars ransom. I was desperate and too tired for this game, as It had become a never-ending saga. I started being careless about myself, I barely could eat something as everything had become without any taste. All I wanted was to get my precious son back, so I reluctantly or stupidly paid the money. I was so angry that my lawyer returned and advised he did not do an immediate swap for my son. He said this is how things are done. I knew straight away even my lawyer was lying to me.

What a well-rehearsed game he was playing too behind my back, and even his secretary played her part well. This lady was a very sexy woman and obviously, she was one of the players in this game. She came to visit me at my Bay Gardens condominium on two separate occasions. On the first visit she was instructed to convince me to pay the ransom, that was when she noticed I had been staring at her arse. Her next move surprised me indeed, when she came over to my reclining chair and started kissing slowly with a taste of candy on her lips. Wow! She was an expert, moreover a true professional, she had been trying to build my trust in her by her giving sexual favors. She knew what to do. I guess she thought or was instructed to do this by my lawyer in the hope I would give more money. I had been given the runaround now for the next two weeks.

When finally, my lawyer's secretary delivered the news in person on her second visit and acted like it was all good news. I was told the ransom had doubled and I just needed to pay another $50,000 American dollars for my son's return. Obviously, I had been scammed; they were never going to release Geoff and really, I was not even sure if Cherry or her lawyer even got any of the first ransom money. Perhaps my greedy lawyer and his assistant kept it all.

I allowed her to give me one more favor, however not a chance were they getting any more money, as how I see it, I paid $25,000 American dollars per favor. They had no intentions of getting my son for me. I was extremely angry, but it did not matter.

It was time now to surrender and move on. About a month after my court hearing, I heard that Charles the drug lord was shot to death in Davao by the police, and Heather had now left the Philippines to America never to return. Perhaps it was their karma, anyway, it did not matter. I had now lost my precious son Geoff. I decided to go back to Hong Kong for a while and do business. My next plan would be then going to Singapore to start my business again, without my thieving partner and so-called friend Gary.

I still felt down and devastated, reminiscing about how much total corruption and lawlessness there was in the Philippines, especially Cebu. This country headed up directly toward the abyss as this land's legal system was utterly in dire straits. As you know that my son and I were Australian citizens, and the mother was an Australian resident, a point I made to no avail to the Australian Embassy who were completely not interested to help me. This was bad to me especially when you do not have anyone in my own country's embassy to rely on. To have a legal system that could change the custody of a child in a contempt of court hearing was illegal. I did file a case against the Judge for ignorance of the law. However, this was also a waste of time. Furthermore, I filed an appeal which also was another waste of time, as this can take up to ten years before I would get a hearing.

Chapter 29

SINGAPORE.

Life always brings you unexpected circumstances. I started expecting nothing; Whatever must come, let it come! I give my life now to the wind. I keep waiting for summer even though life seemed to always bring winter full of storms. I had to be strong; carrying all these heavy things on my shoulders and move on with the next stage of my life and keep busy. After all this, the only thing we can do is surrender to fate and stand watching his badly curved cards playing on in life. The annoyance and frustrations were there, all wishes started being hopeless, remaining in this situation would not add anything to your life except being in despair, weak and all day complaining.

I did not want to complain or drown myself in sorrows. I knew that I had harsh times, but I inversely believe after all the dark days I would scale the mountain watching the clouds moving on, and the light pushing it back to the horizon for a new start and a new phase of my life. I had to cease all this negativity from my thinking, or I would not succeed in my future life. It was time to move on to a new adventure. I decided it is time to explore my next business destination Singapore. I awoke early on an October morning with a refreshing shower and my cup of tea. I headed up to the airport with a big determination. By noon I was on a three-hour Cathay Pacific flight to Singapore where I would restart my business, as I had no idea what was about to happen in the next leg of this crazy life.

After a smooth flight with a good magnanimity as the smile could not leave the face of the hostess, I had been enjoying the flight and the funny movie onboard. I finally arrived in Singapore. I was in a good mood indeed. I headed up to a nice little three-star hotel called Robertson Quay Hotel, which was surrounded by different kinds of shady trees, as it was in the middle of many tall buildings, at the hotel lobby was a cozy, simple cafe. My hotel was near Clarke Quay which in Singapore is maybe the most famous place they have for tourists and locals to hang out, also mingle, and enjoy happy times. Here there are bars and restaurants. Furthermore, this place is on the water, where boats tour the waterways virtually all day and all night. Clarke Quay and nearby Boat Quay could keep you busy for a week.

I had a comfortable night's rest. I then got up early with plenty of energy and anticipation for my new business. I went to check out my new office, where I would launch my business which was at Battery Road in Raffles Place which is the business center of Singapore. It looks here like you are in Manhattan but in Asia. Everyone heading to their work with automatic movements full of modernity. Everything seemed to me was going with harmony like some beautiful guitar melodies but surrounded with modern life. I picked up all the stationery that I had sent by courier before I arrived. I mailed all my letters to begin my business in Singapore again. With a big day full of arrangements and work, I had successfully reborn my business.

It was a very long tiring day; I could not even remember myself until the end of this full-day. I needed shampoo and shave cream and found a shop called Perfect Potion which was an organic supplier of beauty products made from Australia. The shop was perfectly arranged and a relaxing aroma was filling the air with good lighting inside the shop which made it more inviting. I entered with my tired body so quiet to buy what I needed before going back to my hotel. I had been very confused or just like a child when you put him in a new place and he started discovering every corner with a big curiosity.

Then, I heard a soft heavenly voice say "May I help you?" I stood up like a child again gazing at something that fascinated him without showing any reaction. The girl was glowing with a beautiful joyful smile, as you can see this smile through her eyes pull you inside her without giving resistance. I had been following her with my eyes, even in one second, I forgot about the shampoo and shave cream. I only felt through her smile something reminding me of a good memory. I only then said "Yes, I need some shampoo and shave cream". Just after finishing my words, I asked her with a big curiosity in a funny way about her name. She said with a shy smile "Jane". Jane was very friendly and helpful, as well as she has a pretty face. I asked her again in a smarty way "What do you do in Singapore?" with a surprised and confused look in her eyes she then replied "I live here and most of the time I am just working". She finished her words with a big sincere smile that attracted me. I said to myself, I will give it a chance to ask her perhaps to join me for a coffee. Therefore, I invited her anxiously to join me at Starbucks at Clarke Quay after her work. I felt so happy when she agreed.

Time went fast and it was now almost 6pm the time for my meeting with Jane and I was already sitting inside Starbucks drinking my English breakfast tea. The weather outside was perfect that makes you have a feeling of how much you deserve love, how much you are worthy to be loved and dreamed one day to love someone. I had been sipping my tea and savoring every sip still feeling a little anxious while waiting for Jane to arrive. As of now, I mean from moving to Singapore to launch my business, I started to leave the past in the past and was focusing only on the present with big goals to plan for my future. My mind was full of energy and my heart was full of love to establish my life again.

When Jane arrived, I noticed her, shining from the entrance of the cafe, looking for me with her joyful eyes. When she recognized me, she drew a beautiful happy smile on her angelic face. When you meet a beautiful soul, your heart would remember the beauty which has been in the sky flying freely. This beauty takes you to a heavenly level to dance with your heart with a big passion of love. Jane sat down in front of me, as I could not move my eyes from her. I kept silently gazing at her smile, her smile was more beautiful than silence. I became confused when out of nowhere I heard a loud echo inside me telling me, "You will spend the rest of your life with this girl." It was a clear message but I ignored the mysterious voice, as this was utterly impossible, as no way I ever intended to be close to any woman after the life that I had. I ignored and dismissed this mysterious voice.

We got on very well and seemed to have an undeniable connection, this was unfamiliar territory for me. Why all this was happening, I was not sure. I never analyzed or questioned our obvious connection. It seemed that I already knew this girl for years and my heart felt very comfortable with her existence. Perhaps it was from a previous life. How this world works, I have learned nothing is impossible in our mysterious universe. I learned that from several experiences that I had been through. The smallest detail in our being and nature tells you everything is possible, and this girl was one of my beautiful details.

We talked, we laughed, and we were so comfortable with each other, and her smile was consoling me with every sight of her deep eyes. I felt every harmony of her inner beauty. Jane makes me love things differently than I did before. She's a sky full of joy, and a scent of lavender on a rainy day, lighting up my life with a magnificent ray. She is a flourishing flower with her beauty slowly flowing inside my veins. We were sitting in the corner of Starbucks like two teenagers falling in love for the first time in their life. We kissed each other, as we talked a little naughty. One thing led to another and soon we were back at my hotel and Jane stayed the night and the next night. Virtually every time I was in Singapore I would wait until she finished her work. We could be together as we will always be together. We watched movies and toured Sentosa Island with the main attraction the Mythical Merlion which was very crowded with different kinds of people taking pictures with the monument. The view of the park was very calm inside this modern city surrounded by a lot of buildings everywhere. We visited all the places this city had to show.

I arrived at the point where I should not manifest any illusion or any lies in my life. Perhaps, I almost arrived to be careless about everything, but Jane showed up in my life from nowhere. I should be very honest with her and tell her that I do not intend to ever marry again and I do not want any kids. She kept her innocent smile; she did not care or even she did not listen. She just seemed happy for every moment we are together. Jane became a very bad or good habit. By far she was the naughtiest girl I had ever met in my life, and admitted to me she also has an attraction for girls. This was music to my ears, as I do sometimes look at other girls but strangely enough, I had become faithful to just one woman and we seemed to always be in such great happiness together.

Jane was a very simple girl with all her details. I always found simplicity is one of the keys to beauty. Jane has this key, in another word, Jane has the beauty of simplicity. She was not fancy; she was not running after being a Miss World. No makeup, no high heels, and always smiling and happy. She had been working in Singapore for many years and sent all the money she earned to her extended family in the Philippines. I could see by her body language she was not a confident person. Jane, this pretty girl, was just living from day to day and seemed to accept her life this way. In the Philippines, children are taught not to be confident and with the Catholic Church teaching the people to go out and multiply, the country was overpopulated and poverty was a big problem. The children also were brainwashed that they must go and work their life for their parents to share their blessings. My thought was, how many years does a child have to pay for the privilege of being born?

I had been getting concerned. I had been falling in love with Jane. For the first time in my life, I felt I should climb the high mountain to get the beehive for the sweet taste, I wondered about my fate. Jane full of grace, her love makes forgetting other lives. She danced with my heart like the breeze dancing with trees. Yes! I had been with hundreds of women and even married three times, and some of the girls that I had slept with were close to Miss World in beauty, however, I enjoyed the pleasures that a woman's body had to offer. I have to say I never had a deep love for any of them, unlike Jane.

I would hold her hands always, be constantly kissing her when we are together. Also, when we are apart, I would text her with poetic words like poems of Sappho full of love, passion and a lot of affection. She deserved everything, every word that whether someone apart from Jane had read perhaps they would maybe get sick. It seemed the myth about the bow of cupid was actually true and one of his sharp little arrows had penetrated my heart, "Even

I was wearing armor the arrow still went right through", reminding me of the corny song of the late 60's by Leapy Lee called "Little Arrows". Our relationship was blooming like youth, rebellious and very passionate about every phase. Taking all the risks without considering the consequences, like the finest smelling rose that opened its beauty to show the world.

Sometimes, we went for short holidays. The first holiday was in Phuket Thailand, where we spent four days as a sweet pair of love birds. We kept turning kissing each other, we enjoyed every moment. We also went to Bali Indonesia, and had another honeymoon styled holiday and these times were spent being happy, crazy, and naughty. Time just seemed to go so quickly each time there were happy moments full of love and shining like a star in the middle of the night sky. However, I knew once the time was right, we would return but until that time, I just cherished the moment until we had to go back to Singapore.

I wondered about my future now, what it would be? I had been thinking that this girl had given me "Gayuma", which in Philippine language means love potion. Whatever! this naughty crazy man was falling in love with a unique caring girl that seemed almost as naughty as me. This was a really whirlwind part of my life and I just threw caution to the wind and let it happen.

Chapter 30

BANGKOK AND PATTAYA.

It had now been six months since I and my sweetheart Jane had a holiday. This time was spent keeping busy with my business in Hong Kong, Australia, and Singapore. We had planned a holiday again in Thailand where we would have three days in Bangkok and one week in Pattaya. We were very excited for this vacation which would give us a chance that we could explore new memories. The sun was always shining in her eyes and the moon dancing in her smile showing how much she was cheerful for this holiday. Jane said that she has a friend from Singapore working in Pattaya, she mentioned her name was Yuli.

I picked up Jane at Perfect Potion, the organic cosmetic shop where she worked. There was a little drama from her boss. She insisted that we should cancel our holiday because she wanted Jane to continue her work. I cannot believe how people get rude like this, they thought of people as a machine. Sometimes they woke you up from your sleep and sometimes they called from the midst of joyful moments for work! Sometimes you have no choice because you will get fired, there you must go to work with a sad face, cursing everything. I explained rationally to her Chinese Singaporean Boss that Jane had worked six days a week for six months and sometimes twelve hours a day and needed a well-earned break and no way! we were cancelling our holiday.

I said goodbye to this lady boss who looked at me with an angry face and even claimed that I am controlling Jane. I said nothing because I know this kind of person, you better treat them with silence because each time you will say a word, they will show their arrogance like they are ruling the world. I could have said a lot. Imagine my sweet girl had worked long hours for this lady and when she received her salary, Jane has to give back one-third of her salary to the boss in cash which was obviously illegal, but this is how Singaporeans treated overseas workers on work permits. If they dared to make a complaint, the bosses would make trouble. Therefore, nothing was ever said and this was all tolerated by the overseas workers.

We finished this drama by being silent and ignoring the bosses loud demands and just left. We headed up to Changi Singapore Airport in a taxi like a Hollywood movie where the hero picked up his beloved for a new beginning. We were very excited and we forgot her boss once we were on the road toward our heavenly holiday, which was much needed for Jane and I. We arrived at the airport with big enthusiasm, as we rushed our check-in with Cathay Pacific. Time was flashing by so fast and with some great luck at check-in, we were upgraded to Business Class! so once in flight we were now drinking champagne at 36,000 feet onboard a Boeing 777 airplane and Jane was looking at me with her delighted eyes and holding my hand tightly. It was only a two-hour flight, then we arrived at Suvarnabhumi Airport Bangkok which was a very nice airport. It seemed to me like a combination of a mall and museum with great landscape architecture. As usual, there was a long line of people at immigration but we are lucky! we were in business class, so we were able to use the express lane. We were through immigration within twenty-minutes and after collecting our bags we were ready and we were soon in a taxi en-route to our hotel.

We were staying at the JW Marriott in Bangkok which was one of my favorite hotels located near Sukhumvit, a popular tourist district area in this busy bustling city. The hotel was amazing surrounded by glass from all sides with plants and trees in every corner also the black colours added some more luxury to the pattern of the hotel with security guards at the entrance. Inside the hotel was another world. Everything was in the right place and full of elegance, even the decorative lights gave you warmth and a friendly feeling. We checked in for three nights and days in this magnificent hotel with all the legendary luxury the Marriott group provided for their guests. We entered our room; I took a fresh shower then I changed my clothes to get ready for a great tour with Jane.

We spent our time sightseeing and touring the city as this was the first time Jane had been here to Bangkok together, although we had been on a short holiday to Phuket before. The Grand Palace in its entire splendor was our first attraction to visit in the heart of town which was dazzling in yellow contrasting all the colours, which was surrounded with lush beautiful landscaping, with trees that were in patterns which all blended well. The Palace was very crowded with many different kinds of people from every place in the world and also local people. They claimed that the spectacular group of temple-like buildings was the home of the King of Siam since 1782.

We also visited markets and markets of cheap shopping. It seemed that Bangkok was the city of markets and I had to buy an extra suitcase as we had plenty of cheap souvenirs and clothing to carry back to Singapore.

On the second day of our three days in Bangkok, we went down to the River Kwai where this famous bridge or these days a monument was built by the prisoners of the Japanese Imperial Army amongst them were British and Australian soldiers. They were forced to do hard labor without stopping like slaves to build this bridge during the Second World War. The River Kwai tour went for a full day and also stopped at the floating markets on the way, which in itself was a unique and worthwhile stop to visit. It seemed to me like Venice but an Asian version where the boat paddles very slowly because the tiny canal was very crowded. The sides were full of different kinds of markets and some little restaurants, you can see some people shopping and other people eating but everything was moving with a beautiful rhythm. The day was great and a long twelve-hour tour but well worth the trip.

Our final day in Bangkok was spent at the hotel. I was sitting by the pool looking at my beloved through my sunglasses. I was feeling lucky to have this girl beside me. We went swimming under the suns warm heat. After a good day in the swimming pool, we went back to our room to reset and get ready to enjoy Pattaya the following day.

The morning was now upon us, and what is the bigger grace than waking up with an angelic naughty girl beside you, who stole my heart and stole my mind? I started picturing her every sunset, every sunrise with her glowing face. Our spirits were dancing with anticipation for our next exciting trip, we were now on the way to Pattaya, a two-hour trip by taxi which was not that expensive, about 1,200 Baht and Jane was very full of enthusiasm to see her friend Yuli. I am open-minded, however, never envisaged what the next week would bring.

We arrived at the Marriott Hotel Pattaya which has a wonderful garden full of tall palm trees that gave us the impression like we are in Hawaii. The feeling was tropical inside the very magical garden! However, the hotel was in the middle of Pattaya and at the back of the hotel was Royal Garden Plaza which was a nice little shopping mall. I gave Jane a tour of the hotel checking out all the facilities and I could see that the week ahead would be enjoyable. This hotel had many shady areas and was designed for relaxation with a magnificent swimming pool, where I imagined we could hang out and drink a few cocktails at sunset.

We had arranged to meet Yuli at 8pm at Walking Street which was a street where no cars can go from 7pm until 3am and was full of bars and restaurants on every side with a lot of neon lights and loud music could be heard from the discos. Jane and I were sitting at a bar about halfway up the Walking Street. The vibes were lit, Jane was with me like Cleopatra in the Nile, looking for pyramids tonight.

Before we had finished our first Singha beer, which we drank very cold because of the Thailand heat. All of a sudden, a pretty girl showed up with a very sparkling face smiling at Jane, as well for Jane was extremely happy. I could say there is a sort of strong connection between these girls. I saw how they were looking at each other with a big understanding and feelings. Only then after their warm, sweet greeting which was full of kisses and hugs, surprisingly! Yuli looked at me with a cheerful smile and kissed me on the lips. I tasted her sweet moisture on my mouth, as this created a reaction in my pants. This girl was pretty, sweet, also attractive with beautiful skin and all her details were very conspicuous. She drives my imagination to think how tasty it would be to lick this friend of Jane and touch her smooth body slowly with my fingertips. However, I had no idea what was to come that night.

Yuli finally joined us and she added another taste in our evening especially, our vacation in general. We started to drink, talking and laughing. Suddenly, the girls were on the dance floor dancing to the beat of the songs the band was playing and lights moving with the rhythm of the bass. I kept watching these two girls with comfortable eyes, moving with the waves of lights and music. They started kissing so passionately with a poetry way full of love, that makes me figure out many eyes were looking at us with a big curiosity and perhaps envy! Moreover, the more we drank, the less discreet we acted.

A few foreigners were trying to get my girls off me which was disappointing. This is how foreigners are in these Asian countries. They think they can get any girl they want! I said nothing and the ones who approached were totally ignored by the girls. I just kept enjoying the night, chilling with the waves of the lights and music, looking at the girls with a relaxed mood. Luckily! I am a peaceful person. I imagined if I was not, I would see a problem. There were plenty of single girls here in Walking Street, as I wondered what kind of person would endeavor to lure ones that are already taken.

The three of us were having so much fun, as the girls were very lit on the dance floor like a Vodka on the throat, very strong! as their body language dancing were saying everything with a lot of emotions that I catch them with every move. We were beginning to become a little drunk as Jane and Yuli were kissing me slowly with their sweet lips, which I did not complain about! Time moved forward and it was now approaching midnight. I invited Yuli back to our hotel. In my head, I was playing out some fantasies with the two girls.

With a lot of laughter and talking we were finally at the hotel. We entered the room. Once I closed the door, they started kissing each other, I kept smiling at this amazing view. They went to take a shower. They got naked in front of me and I started following this tasty fruit with my eyes. Soon they were showering and kissing each other passionately, then they invited me to join them. These two girls were so naughty and obviously they were lovers before in Singapore.

Jane had no problem sharing me with her friend Yuli for the night. I have to say this was perhaps one of the best crazy sexual fantasy nights come true in my life, similar in many ways to the nights before in London. What a fun exciting night we had. After this amazing night, I could see that we were going to have a great week in Pattaya.

The next morning, I woke up with the smell of sex all through the room. My memory went back to the night before and my thoughts made me excited again. The smell of the room made me realize it was not a dream! It really happened. Then before long, I had a hard erection and I knew we were all tired, however, it did not matter because these girls were wild, young, and lustful. Yuli woke up and started kissing me. I became responsive to her kisses, then Jane also woke up with a beautiful smile looking at us and she started touching Yuli at the same time. We spent the whole morning in bed enjoying fantastic exciting naughty sex again. This was the theme for the week - drinking, dancing, and having more sex.

The week passed very quickly full of amazing days and nights, the music, the good memories, and unforgettable nights that we had like wild teenagers sometimes in the hotel, sometimes in the bar. We did many things - all exciting memories. And now it was the time to leave as we could see the sadness in Yuli's eyes. However, this girl will be ok. We promised that we would return one day to see her. Sooner than later, I hoped, and we penciled in a plan for her to visit Phuket with us next month.

Chapter 31

SINGAPORE RETURN AND ENGAGEMENT.

What we had back in Thailand was more than memorable. I could ride off with these beautiful memories that I made with these naughty girls forever connected with such fantasy that makes me sometimes remember the stories of Egyptian Kings. What we did was very erotic, very sweet, had the taste of passion in it. Nights were quiet enough for me to forget everything even myself in a specific moment. The girls pardon me the cup, and without any hesitation, I took the cup with a big passion and affection toward the world of fantasy that I have in my head. What an amusement! that makes you forget all the harsh things. I and my beloved Jane arrived safely back in Singapore feeling great, after an indelible night like the Persian Poems which cannot be removed from our mind. Thailand "The Land of Smiles" wonderful and it worked and our faces showed the smiles. Also, a new suitcase full from our market shopping.

The next day, Jane had to go back to work; I would stay in Singapore for the next month and work also on my business. We would be apart in the daytime while she was at work but the nights, we would be together. I started missing Jane every second that passed and I counted the days until her work ended. I wanted Jane to finish her work now at months end and be always with me. We had already given her boss a one-month notice to resign by calling her and also by email when we were in Thailand and explore with me wherever life would take us. I fell in love with this girl. I fell into her smile, her pretty face, the way she talks, how she smiles with every word and I fell in love with her pure heart.

We both thought it was the right thing to do for Jane to work one more month until her boss could find a replacement. I decided to do something I have never done as crazy as it sounds. This is how love drives you to be brave to be as a Knight fighting for your girl, taking all the risk to see her smile! Love drives you brave. I know most of the people that knew me and I knew even myself, I had been in many bad relationships that caused me a lot of stress, anxiety, despair, and heartache and cost a lot of money that I was more than crazy. I know Albert Einstein once said "Insanity is doing the same thing over and over again, but expecting different results". I had been married three times before but never asked any of them for marriage. Instead, I had no choice as they all fell pregnant without my approval. I had never been engaged before or asked for a girl's hand for marriage. I was just forced to marry because of their pregnancy.

You cannot imagine how love drives you insane! It started changing suddenly from outside and inside. And this is how far love drove me to become insane. The next day, whilst Jane was at work, I shopped around jewelry stores in Orchard Road and bought a simple but elegant diamond engagement ring set in 18-carat white gold. Now you can see how love drove me crazy, and you can say that I am stupid or you can say the effects of the love potion I suggested I was given by this pretty marvelous girl, who took my heart to another land which is unknown for me! I figured out it is the land of love where you can be lost, and about the sweet taste of her strawberry lips was very epicurean which now occupied my mind, my heart, and my life. It felt right! when your heart keeps insisting on the voice - you should take the call of these voices. The only right way is to follow your heart and Jane was one in a million. I want her always, holding in my arms so tight! I did not get bored or even mad to her. She was never jealous or never got angry. We had known each other now for two years.

These years were very quiet and peaceful, full of happy moments. Sometimes I do not need to explain more or to show more. She just understood me. She took me as I am, and I took her as she is with all her simplicity. I picked up Jane after her work and we had a simple dinner at Starbucks where we first met. Then once we were back in the hotel room, I went down on my knee with my eyes sparkling full of love. I asked this exciting happy simple naughty girl to marry me. The happiness on her face I could never forget. She said "Yes! and Yes! and Yes!" with eyes full of tears, as her heart was dancing in joy as my heart. We were meant to be with each other. She felt to be loved by someone and someone wanted her for just the person she was. I know before she had past relationships but knowing her submissive nature and shyness or lack of confidence, no one truly loved and cared for her like me. She felt chemistry, a connection that she never felt before.

I was not sure where or when we would marry, but both of us wanted a simple unique wedding just for the two of us. After all, this was about me and Jane, not for others. I had been to many weddings before and I felt they were for other people, not for the bride and the groom. By the end of the week, we both had a crazy idea; We agreed we would get married in Las Vegas at the Graceland's Chapel and an Elvis Presley impersonator would do the ceremony.

She rang her family on Skype the night we were engaged. However, I think they did not believe her and thought it was just a big game but no one knows what the past two years were like and no one knows how many things we did together - to understand and believe we were meant to be together; She told her family she was leaving work and also gave her boss one month's notice that she was leaving.

I am not sure if anyone was truly happy for us, I think all were angry that Jane was leaving work. Nevertheless, she had spent five years in Singapore working long hours and gave all her income to her family so as far as I was concerned, she had paid her debt for the privilege of coming to this life. It was now her time to think of herself.

I stayed for the next month with Jane in Singapore, as I started being unable to go away from her. I could say this girl became my addiction. We took the chance to see some concerts of such bands as Chicago which we loved hearing all the old songs of this famous old band. Even though the singers were now in their 60's but they remained cool and played it hard. It was perfect. Journey was on the following week another old band from the 70's. Although they had a new lead singer who was a young Filipino boy, we still enjoyed the music and the atmosphere full of excitement. Even though, I am sure it would have been great to hear the strong fabulous voice of the original lead singer Steve Perry taking nothing away from the new boy. These concerts created many moments of emotions.

We were very lucky again that our life was full of live music, full of freedom, love, and rebellion. Love makes you a rebellious person. All you want to do is to enjoy life to the maximum. How we love How we rebel! And our love was getting bigger and deeper. We took another chance to enjoy two stage shows. The first show was Rock of Ages, a musical which was a nostalgic trip through the Jukebox songs of the 80's. While we had been enjoying the musical, our hearts were also enjoying the melodies. The Jersey Boys "Oh What a Night". We watched this musical at the magnificent Marina Bay Sands. Another memorable night and another unforgettable show we watched together. This musical was in my opinion an absolute classic. This musical traced the story of Frankie Valli and The Four Seasons with all their classic songs performed as well as the originals. These stage shows were truly great and with Jane by my side, the enjoyment we experienced would last forever.

This month in Singapore went fast, and of course full of happy moments and the big wait was now over. Jane now was officially not working anymore for the rude selfish boss. We knew we would soon be flying again back to Phuket Thailand where we had planned to see Yuli, the crazy sexy friend of Jane that I first met in Pattaya. We had a plan for the month's holiday and we were excited after taking my mind back to the last time we saw her.

Chapter 32

YOU ME HER AT PHUKET.

It had been a calm flight aboard a Silk Air 737, with also a perfect landing in Phuket giving a feeling of something good to come. On arrival, Yuli was already there at the airport waiting for us looking extremely exhilarated. She was sure a sight for sore eyes looking as sexy as ever. After the normal hugs and talks as we all acted discreetly at the airport, were soon on our way in a taxi to Patong Beach about a fifty-minute taxi ride away from our airport departure point. Our hotel was the Swiss Hotel which had a very friendly staff who never raised an eyebrow that I was staying with two girls. This hotel was part of the Accor group with its main feature was an outdoor swimming pool on the top floor, which gave a feel of relaxing and changing any mood into the good one.

The hotel was in a perfect location with the view of green hills and the beach which was only a five-minute walk. Once we were checked in our room which had an over full welcoming bowl of fruit and the room was very clean - glowing floors and bathroom with nice colours and more, with a king-sized bed, it did not take long before these two naughty girls began to kiss with passion and their clothes were removed very slowly from their smooth bodies as they began to touch each other very gently and very erotically. Soon I saw tongues and lips kissing full of arousal and passion like soft melodies of Debussy and like butterflies kissing the flowers. Whereas the passion was flowing, I was invited to join this pleasure! It now seemed this is how it would be for the whole month. I merely hoped I could be strong enough to please two lustful girls for the whole month. I was thinking to myself this is a dream, as my desires for these two dream girls were not able to be described so easily.

The first night was very calm and quiet, as we slept early, which enabled us to wake up early. We took a very tasty breakfast and I was sipping on my morning tea while looking at two sweet girls beside me. All this time I was enjoying the smile of Jane and how she added fantasy to my life. After a peaceful morning and delicious breakfast, we went back to our room, dressed in our swimmers, and walked down to the picturesque Patong Beach.

Looking over the water with the sound of the waves and the distant trees dancing with the breeze, a picture came to my mind from back in the year 2003. I could not believe this was the exact spot all those years ago on Boxing Day, a tsunami swept through this beach and killed thousands of unsuspecting people most of which were tourists. I stopped and went back thinking the present time very quickly and stopped thinking like this, as they say now there is a warning mechanism in place to prevent a recurrence of this event or at least people will have a warning and hopefully, no one would be killed if this phenomenon occurs again. We all swam and enjoyed the calm beach waters with the sound of the birds and the shade of palm trees and sunlight kissed our skin. These two crazy-loving girls were swimming carelessly for more than two hours before we agreed to start walking back to the hotel.

Our day was very soothing and relaxing. Everywhere we walked we were always together; I was holding their hands and being sweet. I was always a gentleman with the two beautiful young happy naughty girls and people looked at us and we did not even hardly notice or care. We felt like we are only the three humans on this earth, our soul was running freely. I was proud but humble and I am sure everyone that saw me was either jealous, angry, or disgusted with our relationship but also, many thought it was all okay. Some even gave me the thumbs up with approval.

At night, we explored the bars of Phuket and found a nice Russian bar and the girls had fun joking with the blonde Russian beauties, whilst I just drank in peace with a feeling of total contentment. This was the night we discovered the Moscow Mule drink which is made with vodka, ginger beer, and a little sweet wine which this combination drink became our addiction. This encouraged us to always return each night with excitement to see the beauties and enjoy the cocktails.

We spent a lot of time at Patong beach and there is no better than relaxing on the beach watching the blue sky and the sea with golden sands and green waters. Phuket was an amazing place that does not allow you to become bored at all! It makes you very calm and quiet, and maybe careless about life especially with two girls who were naughty angels. As for the Russian bar, it was adding another taste to the vibes which were very, I can say cinematic with lights and beautiful songs in the background.

The owner of the bar seemed to like our happy nature. He invited us for a tour of the Phuket Islands on his boat and we all agreed as he seemed a trustworthy kind simple man. He picked us up at our hotel the next morning. We felt good when we boarded his luxury boat. Some of the islands we stopped at were Raya Island, James Bond Island to name a couple and the day was total fun. The waters around these islands were clean and clear that you could view the deepest of the water, as everything had been surrounded with a yellow sun decorating the blue sky with the green hills and tall rocks reflecting the colour in the water. Swimming, fishing, and snorkeling was the day's concept on board this boat, as we enjoyed the day. Apart from a little sunburn, we survived our day which went too quickly.

That night, we were back at the Russian bar with our friendly host, as we became very good friends with the staff and especially with the owner who said his name was Boris! if that was his real name because it seemed to be a famous Russian name! Each time we got into the bar he said "Пожалуйста" which means "Please, you are very welcome". When he was saying it, he was gazing at Yuli with a big Russian smile on his face. I could see he was envious, but I also noticed he was seemingly falling for Yuli. Although he knew we were all in a You Me Her Relationship and seemingly happy to be this way so he never crossed the line.

I could see that Boris was a good man as Russian men are very strict and concealing something behind their life. You can see in his eyes the mysterious world that he had but you cannot know what this world is. However, I am pretty sure his past had many secrets that I did not want to know about, because once a Russian started talking about his personal life, you must know he already decided to become your close friend. Moreover, we cannot deny their country was full of Mafia as they are very rebellious with a strong charisma. We have to remember that Russia was once a hard-fisted Communist country and the atrocities of President Stalin were well etched in their history.

We had visited other bars on this party island, as we did enjoy some of the live music performed by cool bands which were mostly Filipino as Thai people have trouble singing as their tongues seem to get twisted speaking English. Mostly our days were spent relaxing at the hotel pool, also keeping fit with morning runs on the beach and gym workouts, furthermore of course sexual pleasure that people could only dream of with two girls.

It was now the last week of our one month in Phuket Thailand and we were all invited to the house or I should say mansion of Boris, our Russian friend, for a Hollywood-like party. There was entertainment and champagne flowing. It was obvious this man, living in the hedonistic world. He is hypersensitive to his potential, settling only for chasing pleasures. I knew these kinds of men, sometimes he wants raspberry, then after a while, he will want a strawberry. This was his addiction inside his world and more obvious, he has money to burn, which makes him being in such an experience without experiencing it to the fullest or even living it. I did not think his bar made enough money to buy all this wealth. Anyway! It was none of my business what he did for a living or what he did experience. At the end of the night or actually sunrise we arrived at our hotel and slept until the next day as overuse of alcohol weakened our bodies to an almost state of paralysis.

This memorable month in Phuket went very fast like thunder. We had to move on and go back to Manila and perhaps a little reality to organize the visa of Jane to America for our planned Las Vegas Wedding. It was very hard to say goodbye to Yuli, but as we say every beginning has an ending. This had to be done, as even though the thought of two wives is fun but not realistic. We did have some love for Yuli, but Jane was the Princess of my heart and she already owned it. The fun of You Me Her had to end.

There was a lot of sadness at the airport when we were leaving like we will not see each other again. With a heart full of longing, we bid a farewell to Yuli as she extended her Thailand visa and was given a job with Boris. Months later, Boris and Yuli had become a couple, as it was more obvious from the beginning that Boris had an eye on Yuli. So, I and Jane were happy to hear this, as they were both good people and we felt they would be a good couple.

Chapter 33

MANILA AND MINDORO ISLAND.

The epic times that we had, still flashing in my mind and how Jane was happy then enjoying the erotic You Me Her nights in Phuket. Those nights were really on fire, flashes from nights in the bar drinking Moscow Mule and music in the air. The sunny days and warm waters of the beach. How could I get enough from this smile from this sweet girl? Her roots started growing up day by day until now she made a Persian garden where Omar el Khayyam had written all his poems. I felt like I was Yves Saint Laurent enjoying his life to the fullest without caring about any consequence or any breaking balance that makes your life unstable. I did not seek for experience, I just ran with the memory of the flashes, ran with people enjoying life and leaving all the past behind. This is sort of Euripides tragedy or poems by Sappho. It is just my life enjoying it to the fullest very slightly like the shade of Icarus wings falling slowly to the earth. I was not willing to fall except falling in love with Jane that was giving me a mythological introspective of love, like Eros and Psyche. The beautiful nights running so fast without perceiving how! we just did enjoy it.

Phuket let us be young and wild again. However, we were now back in Singapore for two final nights, before we were on our way flying back to the Philippines to apply for Jane's American visa for our wedding plans in Las Vegas Nevada with our ceremony which would be performed by an Elvis impersonator and a dream honeymoon trip following the wedding. We were extremely excited and our heart was like a white peacock dancing in a garden full of orange blossoms, as well as we were very delighted to knot our relationship very tightly and become husband and wife. What a feeling! when you finally found your soulmate, the one who completely understands you without expressing it or making an effort. Jane was the one for me, there is no other woman in the world that would like girls and love me and tolerate my open-minded attitude.

After two quiet nights in Singapore, we had now said goodbye to the home of Jane for the past five years. Our flight was with Singapore Airlines onboard an Airbus 330 plane and not long after watching a movie onboard, we had now arrived in Manila, where we stayed at my condo on Manila Bay. The next day after having a good rest and got organized, we went to the American Embassy to apply for Jane's visa which took us the whole day. I was an Australian so I applied for my visa online which was a simple process that took less than one hour. It was a long day waiting for Jane's interview and we were told after her interview that it would take about a week for her visa to be processed.

Rather than stay in Manila, we both developed itchy feet. We decided to catch a bus the next day down to Batangas which is a two-hour trip from Manila, then a boat over to Mindoro Island which was another two-hour trip. My friend Neville who was of South African descent, but had spent most of his life in Australia owned a little resort on the water at a place called Villa Sabang which was at Sabang Beach. A little relaxed seaside village where we stayed for our little holiday away from the hustle and bustle of Manila. I started learning the calmness and peace, without any noises and drama, without any big attraction. I just wanted to enjoy my days with Jane.

It had been a while since I had been here, but it had not changed much just like time stood still. Our first night, we walked over to the main town of Sabang which was only a ten-minute walk, Sabang was a small quiet and simple township where the locals always made us welcome. Also here, there were some little restaurants and girly bars which we planned to visit after dinner to see the entertainment. We went for dinner at Captain Greg's where they served a barbeque type dinner where you choose your steak or chicken or fish and the salad bar was included free.

We enjoyed our healthy delicious dinner with some sweet red wine and relaxed with the rhythm of the ocean feeling its gentle breeze. We then left Captain Greg's and ended up in a girly bar where the young Philippines girls would dance around the poles and some of them were good the way they climbed the poles with very little clothing and looked just like circus acrobats. This was quite entertaining to watch and before I knew it Jane had invited one of the pretty sexy pole dancers to come and sit with us. We were all comfortable and relaxed and having fun enjoying the cocktails together with the beat of the music. We soon found ourselves paying a bar fine to the bar so our new found young friend could join us for the night. She seemed excited and "Madaldal" which meant very talkative as we walked with this girl to our room. She enjoyed the experience of a night with I and Jane. We spoiled her, as she enjoyed all our attention. After all, we had now found it natural to have an extra girl in our bed sometimes.

The next morning, we kissed our little companion bye-bye and we walked over to a place called Big La La Goona as the locals called it, where we planned to eat breakfast. The place was very calming surrounded by nature. On every side, you can find plenty of coconut trees and a calm ocean. These things gave a relief to ourselves after a long night with the pole dancer. I and Jane were needing a very calm day to breathe fine and enjoy the little things the island had to offer. A pleasant twenty-minute walk from Villa Sabang and on the way, we stopped to buy some locally made bracelets and T-shirts for some souvenirs. The sun was brightening, with Jane lighting up my life with her existence like an ocean of love. We had a very peaceful morning with a nice healthy breakfast at the restaurant at Big La La Goona and then walked back to Sabang Beach.

On our way walking back to our hotel, a boat owner approached us asking if we would like to hire him and his boat for the next day. He said "Would you like to visit White Beach and island hop for the day?". This sounded like a great idea, so we both said "Yes!" with big excitement. We then agreed on a price with the respectful man, we arranged to meet up at 8am the next morning at the front of Villa Sabang. We did spend a relaxing day, as the night came very fast, we just did our usual things with love and peace. It was heaven on earth with Jane.

After a good night's sleep, the morning came around, and sure enough, here was the boat, as the owner had been waiting for us and ready for our days travelling around this island of Mindoro. The first stop was at Puerto Galera, the main town on Mindoro Island which was a very quiet town with an amazing beach, with many souvenir shops at the water's edge. This was a short stop and soon we were back in our little bunker boat which is a small wooden boat with a roof or canopy made also of wood and two long bamboo poles on each side to avoid the boat tipping over. The small diesel motor was at the back where the driver sat and navigated with a wooden rudder.

We were now on our way to White Beach, a further forty-minutes trip around the next bay. We had a great day at White Beach which is beautiful, nice and quiet spot with no crowds and very peaceful. It is a simple little township with many restaurants and small markets, as the locals were very cheerful people. We were greeted on the beach by two old ladies with baskets of fruit and they skillfully made us a wonderful delicious healthy lunch. After sitting and spending the time relaxing at this amazing place especially with Jane was a daydream. We left White Beach after two enjoyable hours and set sail again for Sabang Beach, and on our way back, we stopped at another couple of small islands and snorkeled until the day turned to night and the darkness was upon us. We then set sail home for the final time sunburned and tired from a great day out.

Eventually, after a few more days at this peaceful relaxed location, we received a phone call advising Jane that her American visa was approved. We were both so ecstatic that drove us to celebrate the last night on the island dreaming of our upcoming marriage. The next day we made the trip back to Manila, then caught a taxi straight to the American Embassy and arrived just in time to collect her passport. When Jane opened her passport to check her visa, I saw pure happiness on her face, as her eyes were sparkling with joy. We were very impatient and excited for our trip ahead to the USA which I had never been before. We were planning our dream trip of a lifetime and had booked in to be married in The Graceland's Chapel on August 16 which coincidentally as we found out a year later was the anniversary of the death of the King "Elvis Presley".

Our flight was due to leave Manila on August 14. We were all set now and spent a few days in Manila excited and patient. We also planned our honeymoon in the USA which also included a cruise from Miami Florida. All in all, our wedding and dream honeymoon were very organized and we were ready to leave.

Chapter 34

LAS VEGAS-OUR WEDDING.

It felt like I have lived to love Jane. I started feeling loved as she filled every emptiness inside me with her devotion. She is so much fun to be with and so wild. She has poetry shining around her as she took all the past lives out of the context with all our holidays and beautiful moments that we had together. I will always take her hand and will not let her go. I wanted her as she is, I wanted her as pure simple Jane.

The day now arrived for our USA trip and soon we lifted off from Ninoy Aquino Manila Airport on a Cathay Pacific plane, with a long journey ahead to our fantasy wedding and holiday. We were completely prepared with contentment in our soul, as we were very enthusiastic like every newlywed who are in love. I kept turning to see the pretty face of my future wife. Even though the flight was long, travelling and being with this sweet girl, the time would not matter. I started being careless about time. The only thing that I now care about is my life with Jane. Here we were now eventually touching down at Las Vegas Airport. I was still feeling like this was another dream. I felt my life had become now full of fantasy dreams replacing my past nightmares that seemed for now to be just a distant bad memory. Jane is my aether, filling my soul like sweet melodies dancing in harmony with the beauty.

After a short ride, we reached the Las Vegas Strip with all the dazzling bright lights in this famous town, shining bright and lighted signs flickering in a spectacular way that makes you remember a happy memory or just that gives you a notion of a good future. This place was just how I did imagine it, after seeing this from many movies that we had watched in the past which were set in Las Vegas. We checked into The Cosmopolitan Hotel right in the middle of the Vegas Strip and this place had excitement written all over it, with an amazingly well-presented room, very clean, very spacious and the view overlooked the Bellagio Fountain and the famous Vegas strip. I and Jane were buzzing with anticipation of what was ahead.

It was now 11pm and we went to register for our upcoming marriage as here in Las Vegas Nevada the registry office is open 24-hours a day. The process was very easy and we were now relieved that everything was organized for the 16th at The Graceland's Chapel. We then checked out the excitement of the Vegas Strip for a while before returning back to our hotel room at 1am. It was a long day that seemed to last two days, maybe because we had gained almost a day in transit as Manila time is 16-hours ahead of Las Vegas time. We still had one more day until our wedding, so we now booked online to organize a trip up to the Grand Canyon tomorrow or actually it would be later today. Totally exhausted, we now slept.

Later that morning, we went downstairs half asleep to the lobby. Our van was on time picking us up at our hotel at 7am. We heard the driver calling our names which woke us up as we dozed off in the lobby. We were then ready and raring to go for our all-day tour. Our first stop was Hoover Dam named after the famous FBI Boss of the 60's, named Edgar Hoover and this was a huge concrete dam in the Black Canyon of the Colorado River on the border of Nevada and Arizona. We truly marveled at this gigantic construction and it whetted our appetite for the next stop.

Arriving at this amazing marvelous Grand Canyon, and what a sight to behold a huge Canyon with a deep drop to the bottom and no safety fences.

We were startled seeing young Japanese tourists sitting on the rim of this sheer drop with their feet hanging over. Not us! We kept back from the rim and took the safe and sensible option which was the Skywalk which allowed us to be directly above the deep deep canyon, with this sight taking away our breath. One lady on the Skywalk had her straw hat blown from her head and we watched the hat slowly slowly, but surely drift below until it was out of sight of normal human eyes, somewhere near the Canyon's floor. We checked out this magnificent wonder of the world, this canyon is a natural formation that took millions of years to form. The vast size being 10 miles wide and over 1 mile deep and runs for close to 277 miles long with the Colorado River running through with white water rapids.

We kept gazing at this deep and marvelous Canyon and hearing our echoes that sounded like a piece of classical music. Even if you have such a problem, it would not be bigger than this place right here. I found the occasion to express my love to Jane, by saying "My love for you was deeper than this Canyon." Jane after hearing these words, hugged me like a candle in the wind, with her big beautiful smile. We both then laughed at how corny I had become, I was then also hoping no one else overhead my words to Jane. After a delicious lunch, we were soon on our way home back to our hotel to prepare for our big day tomorrow.

We were both worn out but the dopamine and a lot of happiness make us forget even ourselves. Although we had not rested since we left Manila, however it seemed we were surviving on pure adrenaline from our enthusiasm. We slept early, nevertheless, my sleep was restless, my heart merely was waking all night with big inner happiness.

The morning of our wedding was here. I bounced out of bed and woke my sleepy wife to be and we then went to the local Starbucks for a light breakfast and coffee. After a light breakfast, which was all I needed to eat, my stomach was full of adrenaline or like butterflies flying inside. I was a little nervous while waiting for the next few hours to pass before our ceremony. We went back to our room, we dressed in our wedding clothes.

Jane had a simple long-sleeved white dress which fitted her sexy body perfectly, as her soft skin like bronze and her hair like cashmere and shining like a precious diamond. The dress was simple but perfect with high silver heeled shoes matching well. She looked simply beautiful and as for me, my attire was blue jeans which were my dream to wear at my wedding, and a light black long-sleeved shirt and white tie. I was feeling "Gwapo" which is Spanish for Handsome. We were very happy, just simple big happiness. We then found a taxi without any problem, as the driver knew the chapel. We were now on our way to be married by the King Elvis Presley, well! At least an impersonator. The friendly taxi driver wished us very good moments and a life full of happiness and joy. He asked for a tip for good luck as he said this was a tradition in Las Vegas, I smiled at the taxi driver and because of his convincing words, I handed him an extra $10 note.

We were at The Graceland's Chapel and waiting for our ceremony, taking photos and selfies at the front of the chapel. We were ready to begin. It was just me, Jane, Elvis and the cameraman. The girl that I decided to continue my life with had everything. I wanted her from the bottom of my heart, Jane was a very special and unique girl and my decision was right when I said she is the one. Jane becoming now the queen of my heart, crowning her love inside me.

Now! our ceremony began. Elvis was about 7-feet tall or at least 6.5-feet tall wearing a sparkling gold blazer, brightening more because of his black hair. He was wearing shiny big rings on almost all of his fingers with his white teeth and blue eyes. For a while I wondered, is this really Elvis? but if you gaze too long you will see how this man was a very good impersonator. Also, I do not think Elvis was that tall.

He walked Jane down the aisle of the chapel to where I was standing at the altar, while he was singing his famous song "Can't Help Falling in Love" I joined the chorus, as he joined our hands. Next, we repeated our vows after Elvis whilst looking into each other's eyes. Elvis was now singing "Love Me Tender" increasing with it the true feeling of the ceremony, only then after this song, I placed the ring on Jane's finger and I said with eyes full of love and affection "I promise that I will always Love you Tender, never have a Suspicious Mind, never leave you in Heartbreak Hotel, and always be your Hunka Hunka Burning Love". Jane then placed the ring on my finger and said the same vows to me and then we were pronounced husband and wife.

We kissed with a lot of affection, as our hearts and eyes were crying with big happiness which could not be described by words, with a lot of kisses to seal our promises. After our vows were done, we then danced out of the chapel singing "Viva Las Vegas!" Many would say this was a very corny ceremony, however not to us! We said our vows with solemn belief and the happiness of the event were written on our cheerful smiling faces and now we were Mr. and Mrs. for life.

We then went back to our hotel in a white Limousine which was part of the package from a memorable ceremony full of love and affection. Which would be "Always be on my mind". Jane loved me without any complexity without any expectations. She just loved me as I am and I promised myself to love her every second and get "Lost in Love" with her without caring about the consequences or what fate would bring. My life was like a desert before Jane. She entered my life like a beautiful rain, flourishing all my sides, as in a period I felt like I was a man without a fate, now Jane my only fate, melting my heart with her pure heart and sweetness with all the wonders from her, with all honesty and without any limits for her love.

She melted me with her smile. I loved her above everything. Back in our room, we consummated the marriage and then ordered a bucket of ice for our bottle of Moet champagne, which we had bought for the occasion and soon we toasted our wedding. The champagne put the newlyweds in a good mood. We then ventured downstairs, spending our wedding night at the hotel-casino playing blackjack and drinking some free corona beers which were complimentary whilst we were playing. We left after two hours winning $100. We kept that money and never returned to the gambling tables until we left; After all, we wanted to leave Las Vegas winning, as I am sure, we would be a minority that achieved that feat, we were both extremely happy with our little win.

On our last day in Las Vegas, we savoured the shrimps for lunch with the ice-cold corona beer at the Bubba Gump's restaurant, made famous by the movie of the same name, and then spent the day checking out some of the famous Las Vegas spots on the Strip. Caesars Palace was the first stop; this casino hotel is well known for its famous boxing events over the years with its large dancing water fountains. MGM was the next stop and this hotel-casino was also famous for its world-class concerts and shows. Next to Circus Circus with its amusement park and waterslides. Lastly, the Venetian which was built on the site of the old Sands Hotel.

We could have spent a week with all the hotels and casinos in this wonderful city of bright lights where people have won and lost fortunes over time. However, we felt we had seen enough, and it was now time to return to The Cosmopolitan Hotel and rest and pack for our next flight tomorrow where we would stop at San Francisco which was a short flight less than two hours away from Las Vegas.

Chapter 35

HONEYMOON IN THE USA.

Our flight from Las Vegas landed on time at San Francisco California Airport, excited to be in this famous city. Jane was holding my hands, as I was tightly holding her hands with feelings of love, as we were freezing upon arrival. The first thing we needed to do was to buy something warm to wear. We found a hooded jacket at the airport souvenir shop, then we quickly put them on our cold body with huge relief. Jane looked like a cute kitten in this hooded jacket. I remember reading the words of Mark Twain the famous American writer who said "The coldest winter I ever spent was a summer in San Francisco". Mark Twain was absolutely right and these words literally described the conditions, and now I know what he meant.

Crossing the Golden Gate Bridge to the city made us remember the words from the song "Be sure to wear a flower in your hair". We visited the hippy and flower power area of town and remembered how peaceful it would have been in those days. Next onto Chinatown, from here we took the cable car to Fisherman's Wharf where a great rock band was playing. Everyone was having their own party, dancing, singing with the band, clapping or sometimes screaming. It was a very cool and happy atmosphere in this flower power cold city. We ate some delicious Clam Chowder whilst looking across the Bay at the notorious Alcatraz. San Francisco had a lot to offer but we were now heading back across the Golden Gate Bridge to the airport for our next stop in Hawaii.

Hawaii was a reasonably long flight from San Francisco aboard our Virgin America 737. No worries for the travelers! Jane was laying her head on my shoulder and Me, I was enjoying the beautiful scent of her hair. I was holding her in my arms like we're two love birds in the tree caring for each other. On our first day in Hawaii, we explored the beaches of Waikiki and the Hula Dancing. We discovered a Napa Valley red wine called Barefoot in small bottles at the ABC convenience shops that are plentiful on the island. Each night I would sit on the beach with my dear wife, simultaneously while Jane was enjoying the sunset, I was enjoying her company. She entered my life with closed gates to my heart, and she did open them only with her smile and simplicity. The sunsets were fantastic as we got "Lost in love" in a foreign place. When the sun would go away, I would still see Jane. She is my sun that lights up my life. We cherished these moments to the fullest, just wasting time with our newfound red wine.

The famous places like Sunset Beach, Pipeline and Waimea Bay where the world's best surfers would come to enjoy the winter swells and ride waves sometimes up to thirty-feet high. No trip would be complete here without a visit to Pearl Harbour which was a sad but true fact this place was bombed by the Imperial Japanese Navy on December 7, 1941. Hawaii was heaven on earth, and with Jane, its mamamia! Jane added happiness and light soft soul into each place, each event, each condition. One of the powers of Jane was capable of turning your sad mood into a happy mood in a few seconds. After our four-day trip, it was time to leave as tomorrow we were off to L.A.

Los Angeles California, this city was written a lot by fabulous American poet and writer Charles Bukowski. Not only by

Bukowski, but you can also find several beautiful songs written about this city and more largely about the state of California with the poetic style of life, how people ride the melodrama of this city. We arrived at Tom Bradley Airport, which was a very busy airport, although we did survive the crowds. Soon we were aboard an uber car which would drop us off at the Residence Inn located in Downtown L.A.

The Metro Train Line was just a ten-minute walk from our hotel so on our first day in L.A, we caught the train up to Santa Monica Beach which was close to Venice Beach and only a forty-minute train trip. We hung out here all day after hiring a couple of push bikes for getting around on the beach paths followed by lunch at Bubba Gump's whilst enjoying ice cold Corona beers. Next day we caught the metro in a different direction up to Long Beach, another forty-minute trip. Exploring the famous Queen Mary which was a luxury boat built by the same people as Titanic and had a similar look. It was parked here after its final trip from Southampton London in 1967 and is now a floating hotel.

To complete our L.A trip, Hollywood and the Walk of Fame which we explored after our morning hike through the Hollywood Hills stopping at the Space Observatory on our grueling steep walk. This observatory was made famous by the 1955 James Dean movie "Rebel without a Cause". Jane was like Venice Beach so beautiful and insane, as she was singing with her eyes. I was fond of her sweet lips and holding her close to me from time to time. Jane in California was like a solo guitar, very poetic and full of feeling without expressing her music to the outworld. We fell in love with L.A however, we had many places still to explore in this great country. Tomorrow, we would be off again flying to Seattle.

Seattle is a small city, two days to see what we could in this sleepless city. First to the top of the Space Needle then we came across the Duck Boat tour which was a ninety-minute land and water tour of the city. The tour guide gave a great comedy tour with his bald head using different wigs in every story. The next morning, we went for a special coffee at the original Starbucks that was open in 1971, as this cafe would always relate to such memories in my life. While I am on the cusp of changing, I found myself all the changes started with Starbucks coffee. I love how things go without expecting it, without any plans, you just go with the flow and let it flow.

My pretty wife was enjoying Seattle with happiness and joy to discover each place with a big curiosity on her face. I am very proud of her to take and be with her in all these places. We then found the King Street train station and bought our tickets for tomorrow's Amtrak train trip to Vancouver which was about three hours from Seattle.

Chapter 36

CANADA, BAHAMAS AND MORE OF USA.

We woke-up in a great mood for travel. Early morning, we were on our way to our next destination Vancouver Canada, travelling aboard the Amtrack train which was a picturesque journey passing lakes and waterways. Our first night in this wet cold city, we went to a local bar and drank some nice sweet wine. The next morning, we dedicated our day to walk around the famous Stanley Park which is a 405-hectare public park and is mostly surrounded by water. Capilano Suspension Bridge Park, where we discovered the parklands after crossing the suspension bridge which crossed the Capilano River in the Northern district of Vancouver. This city was worth the visit and we were looking forward for our next stop for tomorrow.

Toronto has a three-hour time difference from Vancouver, we arrived at night time. We simply checked into the Courtyard Marriott and whilst chatting in bed about tomorrow plans, we fell asleep with our heavy bodies which were tired from traveling, but we still have the young energy, as well as for our curiosity which was getting bigger and bigger, especially for Jane who was fascinated by every place like a child observing everything.

Early next morning, a tour bus picked us up to see the famous Niagara Falls. We marveled at the sight of this magnificent waterfalls. We sat in a café sipping coffee and eating homemade maple on pancakes for hours staring at the falls. Watching the water flow very charismatic made me remember how I was just a drop of water before meeting Jane, how this drop of water falling from the sky simply becoming in the wild river flowing strongly towards the great lakes. This was us, we were two rivers of love flowing inside each other, as we started becoming just one instead, we were just one drop away from each other. I finally found her, and I am very grateful to have her by my side. What a magical feel the falls radiated to us.

We had a late return to the hotel and just slept. Upon wakening we explored this great city and all of the historical sights of Toronto. We fitted in well with the naughty goings-on at the back of our Hotel at Yonge Street at night. We even had a visit to the swinger's club at this naughty Yonge area. Inside this place, some unusual things were happening, but we were both open-minded and nothing shocked us! All in all, it was fun inside the swinger's club, and even though we did not mix much, we merely enjoyed this club that had live sex shows for all patrons to view. It seemed in this club anything goes. thus, we fitted in well to the concept and left with another new experience of life's wonders.

Miami was our next stop, the city of upmarket people and famous beaches which I felt were similar to the Gold Coast of Australia. We had a few days here before we were to board our cruise to the Bahamas onboard the Royal Caribbean ship called "Empress of the Sea". Our planned cruise to Cuba was suddenly changed because of new laws introduced by the US banning cruises to Cuba. Yes! We were disappointed as we were looking forward to seeing this interesting country which had been the source of the greatest men like Fidel Castro and Che Guevara. We vowed to one day visit Cuba at another time. At least we were still able to enjoy Little Havana in Miami, which was a taste of Cuba where we did explore the streets of Calle Ocho and tried Cuban coffee, and danced to Cuban Latin music.

Before long, we were on our way pulling out of Miami for a seven-day cruise. We started talking to the other passengers on deck watching as the ship pulled out from the shore. I had come to realize here in the USA people are friendly, happy, and amicable to all walks of life. This cruise was a trip where we saw pink shorelines and silky white sands with first stop the Grand Caymans, home of the Margaritaville Resort. We walked along the sandy white beach, holding each other's hands and adoring life as a married couple. We went for a swim, having fun under the hot sunbeams, before returning a little sunburned.

Belize next stop, well not much happened here and maybe the highlight was talking to an old man that was perhaps 100 years old with his long thick blonde braided hair that I doubt had been washed for at least ten of his years. Then onto Costa Maya Mexico before our final stop Key West Florida and without a doubt this day was the highlight of our cruise, where people seemed gay and free with nude painted bodies everywhere to be seen. Once our cruise arrived back in Miami, we then had to move quickly to the airport for our flight to New Orleans Louisiana.

We checked into our hotel which was the Town Place Suites in Canal Street, New Orleans. At sunset we found the famous Bourbon Street where we drank a few too many Grenades, which is one of the famous cocktails they serve there. These cocktails were served in of course a grenade-shaped container and after a few of these addictive drinks, we were rocking. This truly is a fun party place, as the Jazz bands played very lit with the melodies of a piano and soft trumpets playing and very low beats of drums in the background giving such a romantic atmosphere. The bands played at many bars and even on the streets making the experience livelier.

We staggered home from Bourbon Street in the early hours of the morning. However, surprisingly the next day we felt ok! It was a quiet relaxed day where we sat in the cafes and allowed ourselves to become addicted to the Beignets. On our last day we took the old-fashioned paddle steamer up the famous Mississippi River enjoying the jazz music band onboard in this city of old-time music. The cemeteries here in New Orleans had amazing stories to tell, this was also the burial place of the famous Voodoo Queen Marie Laveau.

We flew from New Orleans to our final stop, New York. Another smooth trip as it seemed the American pilots were well trained compared to some other countries. Soon we arrived at LaGuardia Airport. New York or The Big Apple as it is known, is very attractive, which is shaped by the waves of immigrants. New York is very unique like no other! as its influence radiates to every corner of the globe. Each street, each place it seems very familiar through a movie and song.

We strolled around the Central Park which is on 750 acres of land on Manhattan Island. We also caught a Ferry trip to the Statue of Liberty which is in New York Harbour. We watched the Phantom of the Opera on Broadway, as I am not sure if it was the red wine or the music! However, we both had a good sleep watching the show. Following the show, we were energized. We hung out at Time Square until late at night. I and Jane also explored the 9/11 monument and museum where the crazy terrorists crashed two planes into the towers on September 11, 2001. Last but not the least, we went to the top of the famous Empire State Building which was opened in 1931 and was the tallest building in the world at the time of completion with an observatory on the 86th Floor. While at the top we remembered the movie

Sleepless in Seattle where this building was the location of the last scenes of the romantic classic.

Chapter 37

LONDON AND EUROPE.

The moment in time we were both dreading was here, the date for our return back home to Australia. I now felt like Marco Polo travelling with Mrs. Jane Polo after our expedition through the USA and Canada following our dream wedding. Whilst waiting for the check-in counter to open at JFK Airport, the two of us suddenly had second thoughts about ending our honeymoon. Jane then said "I wish we could keep travelling" the same words I was thinking to say to her. Instead of transiting in London and then onto Australia, we changed our ticket for a stopover at Heathrow Airport for an extra month's stay to discover Europe.

On arrival at Heathrow, we excitedly collected our bags, went through the immigration, and were ready to explore whatever we could in this massive continent of Europe. I missed London and remembered all the good memories I had here from my last visit. This time, I was with my wife Jane which London would be very different than the last time. Next thing we were on the Heathrow Express to town. We booked a small hotel in Earls Court not far from the tube stop. I cuddled my sweet wife under the sky of London then slept feeling very contented.

We only woke up with the morning light breaking into our room. Now we were full of zest and in a good mood especially Jane to see London Town. The best way to sightsee here is the famous open-air red Hop on Hop off bus. This bus travelled around the city showing us the sights, visiting all that was possible in the time we had. In this time, we also attended two classic musicals Miss Saigon and Mama Mia at the West End Theatres.

Cannes in the French Riviera was the next destination where we stayed at the JW Marriott Hotel, which is located in the heart of this festival town, only a few steps away from the beach with an amazingly breathtaking view of the bay. Just as we checked in, we quickly put our bottle of champagne in a bucket of ice and began to get the feel of this millionaire's paradise. The sweet French champagne put us in a great mood, and we were enjoying this playground with all the rich and famous people in this small but eloquent little beach town that has a history of The Cannes Film Festival. We also found a nice old-fashioned movie theatre where we watched the movie version of Jersey Boys. A few days was enough in Cannes, and we were now ready to leave for Gay Pari better known as Paris the city of love. The best way of getting there was by train, with amazing views along the way, showing the French countryside and the beauty of this country. It seemed like a dream to be travelling to Paris and Jane was ecstatic and full of enthusiasm to see Paris.

Our train was soon pulling into Gare Du Nord Station Paris mid-afternoon and excitement was circulating through our bodies. Soon we checked into the Marriott Hotel in Champ Elysees, which is the main famous street in Paris and also headed you up directly to Arc de Triomphe. We went straight to the Eiffel Tower. It was cold as only three days away from Christmas. We lined up freezing cold in drizzling rain for two hours until finally, it was our turn to board the breathtaking elevator ride to the top of the tower. I held Jane close to me and we kissed while looking around the majestic view right across Paris.

This view was worth the two hours wait. After only thirty minutes we had to descend back down the elevator gleeful, feeling the cold weather. We then spent the next two days sightseeing at all the Paris sights. The Louvre Museum was our first stop, even though there was a long queue, we were able to view all the impressive and skillful art, especially the most famous Mona Lisa painted by the genius Leonardo Da Vinci. We explored all the historical Paris landmarks visiting Notre Dame, Montmartre, Arc de Triomphe, and our favorite place Moulin Rouge. Our Christmas in Paris will always be an unforgettable memory for the rest of our lives.

Paris was a very poetic, romantic city full of love, beautiful historical buildings, fashion and culture. Jane was very happy to discover French with a big passion to know each phrase, as she learned how to say I love you in French "Je t'aime" It was very funny to hear these words came out from her sweetest lips, as I cut her words with a French kiss then saying "Je t'aime Aussi". We left Paris with a heart full of French love, full of art and new culture.

Our next train trip was to Amsterdam Netherlands, arriving late in the afternoon. We walked around the streets here where the air was full of Marijuana or Cannabis where the smoke made us feel a little dizzy. These substances were served legally in the clubs which were plentiful in the city. This was not for us as we preferred to be naughty and talk to some ladies of the night standing in front of their little rooms, displaying their sexy bodies for all to see. We left the city of bicycles before flying off to Barcelona Spain, arriving in time for the New Year's Celebration.

We had a day before the New Year's, so we explored Barcelona with amazement. Architect Gaudi had his footprint all over this quiet peaceful place. His most famous building was the Basilica de la Sagrada Familia which was never finished before his tragic death. New Year's celebration in

Barcelona was so much fun with free champagne together with green grapes as their tradition for the countdown and we partied all night with amazing fireworks over the dark sky at midnight.

Next, we arrived at Fiumicino Airport Rome, the Eternal City as it was once known. We ventured to the Trevi Fountain a short walk from our hotel, where we threw a coin each and made our wishes hoping they would one day come true. Jane was truly wondering about my wish, but I said in my mind Jane is only my wish. I smiled, as I kissed her with affection in a naughty way. "While in Rome, we ate like the Romans." Eating the same food every day, as every restaurant served the same foods, and we always washed the pizza and pasta down with some Italian sweet red wine. So much to see and do in this city, and so much history to discover with the highlights of the next two days visiting the famous Colosseum where in ancient times the Gladiators would fight to the death in front of huge crowds and the Emperor of Rome. The Sistine Chapel was also wonderful with Michelangelo's paintings in magnificent view all over the Catholic Church's ceiling.

Leaving Rome, one of the most wonderful cities in Europe which is full of great history, we had a short stop in Berlin. Here we had a river cruise sampling the German beer Hoegaarden. The most interesting place was Checkpoint Charlie as it was called. It was the crossing point of the famous Berlin Wall which divided East and West Germany with the soviet communist rule in the East and Freedom on the West. This was another reminder of human stupidity which took my memory back to my visit to the North Korea border.

Berlin was a rushed trip but at least we tasted a little of the city. Our next flight was to Copenhagen Airport Kastrup. Copenhagen which is in Denmark, was a quiet peace-filled place where in the evening we would sit in the city center and drink the local beer that we purchased from the 7Eleven shop and listen to the Buskers singing.

Late in the afternoon we left Copenhagen by boarding a nineteen-hour overnight Ferry to Oslo Norway. Our comfortable cabin put us in a state of "Hygge" and with the swaying of the boat, we slept well. After disembarking the ferry in Oslo, we were wandering early morning in our new surroundings. Remember here in Scandinavia in July the sun only goes down for four hours a night. Norway was a quiet place and maybe the best things to do here was to visit the Kon-tiki and Viking museums.

Stockholm Sweden was a four-hour train trip from Oslo. There was much to see in this city known as the Venice of the North due to its abundant waterways. The Abba Museum with old videos, and what a nostalgic place with videos and memorabilia from the 70's. It was now time to make our way to the cruise ship for our much-anticipated seven-day cruise of the Baltic Sea.

Chapter 38

BALTIC CRUISE AND RUSSIA.

This would be our second time to cruise. The interior of the ship was superb and although our room was a small cabin it did not matter as it had plenty of room for us to feel comfortable. We sat on the top deck sipping red wine and thrilled for what was ahead over the next seven days onboard "The Serenade of the Sea". We set sail with a cheer as we toasted our cruise ahead before returning to our cabin.

The ship had now set a course to our first stop Visby Sweden and upon awakening we were docked ready to disembark. It was a twenty-minute walk to the center of this medieval Hanseatic town. The cold wind and rain then forced us to spend the rest of the day in a quaint coffee shop. After about four hours the rain stopped just long enough for us to see a bit of the town and walk back to the ship for dinner. Next stop Tallinn Estonia, which was in many ways similar to Visby with its medieval architecture. We spent our day in the Old Town with a walking tour starting from the town hall before tasting some A. Le Coq beer in the Sigmund Freud Bar before we headed back to the ship.

After two nights onboard, we then anchored for two days in Saint Petersburg Russia with all its history. The beautiful blonde Russian girls were our favorite attraction and here we spent our two nights off the ship staying in a local hotel where in the daytime we toured and at night we had fun with the Russians in the nearby night club.

Last stop Helsinki Finland, where we walked for hours from the port to the town. We were told the way to town was to follow the path around the lake. The pattern for the day was walking as once we arrived in town, we then went for a long walking tour before boarding a local bus to return to the ship.

After our final night's sleep, we arrived early the next morning back in Stockholm, Sweden. Here we had one night sleeping in an old 747 plane at Arlanda Airport that had now been transformed into a hotel called Jumbo Stay where we ate our dinner on the wing!

We left Stockholm early morning with Singapore Airlines flying onto Moscow Russia. Once through immigration, we made our way out of the airport terminal. We then found a local bus about a 100-meter walk from the terminal, which took us from the airport to the Metro where we boarded a train that stopped at a station closest to our destination, the Marriott Grand Hotel. The first day in Moscow we walked down to Red Square. We fell in love with Moscow, even the train stations were like museums with the ceilings painted and the statues sculptured by skillful artists.

I have to say the Russian girls were beautiful and friendly and they were our highlight. Yes! the paintings and sculptures were nice but the girls were stunning. I could talk all day and night about this city, where the people were friendly and the girls were beautiful and the hotel we stayed in was a magnificent relic from the 18th century.

On our second day, we were sitting in Subway sandwich bar eating and noticed a stunning young blonde girl sitting across from us. Jane smiled at her and was surprised when she smiled back. Jane invited her to join us and the girls seemed to be happy talking together. It was late afternoon so Jane invited the girl named Sonia for a drink with us, as we found a bar not too far from our hotel.

I was enjoying a good conversation with the locals in the bar while Jane and Sonia were now holding hands. Jane then said, "I want to take Sonia and show her the hotel". I replied "Ok! good idea". I just stayed contented in the bar while the girls were gone for maybe two hours and when Jane and Sonia arrived back to the bar. I had an idea the girls were doing a little more than talking in the room. Jane told me later that she wallowed every bit of the beautiful Sonia, which made me pleased and I gave her a smile of approval. Over the next week, they met again. I also got to know some beautiful and friendly Russian girls which was one of my life's remarkable experiences.

Sadly, our travel time came to an end. We had a memorable time, collected unique souvenirs and photos in each place we visited. Jane was giving a special feel to my life that never allowed any feelings of boredom to surface. It was time to leave Moscow. Imagine travelling the world for months on an endless honeymoon. The memories we created on our travels can never be taken away. These escapades and our exploits were now permanently etched in our minds forever.

My life had now travelled full circle over the past twelve years, from bad relationships and marriages to devils, to finding my true angel. I went from jail and expensive court cases, to finding peace and harmony. I stumbled but did not fall, even sometimes I thought there was no point to continue. This world had given me extraordinary fantasies, it also gave me mental hardships and devastating heart breaks. I accepted the bad times and enjoyed the good, as this is the roller coaster ride of life when you take chances and explore. One thing is certain, I learned what is life and I believe that taking chances even how stupid they turn out to be, is better than just existing in a comfort zone with regrets from not searching.

Now today, what started as only a dream became reality. I now live with true contentment, and I am amazed that life guided me to be with my beautiful wife. Now for the past ten years together, I had found harmony and happiness in life. My karma was to find my true destiny Jane and our little precious daughter, Gem.

THE END

www.ingramcontent.com/pod-product-compliance
Lightning Source LLC
Chambersburg PA
CBHW050308010526
44107CB00055B/2157